Presented To:

From:

Date:

Stop Waiting...Start Winning!

Stop Waiting...Start Winning!

10 Essential Principles — to — Live your vision **NOW!**

Teresa Hairston

DESTINY IMAGE₀ PUBLISHERS, INC.

P.O. Box 310, Shippensburg, PA 17257-0310

"Promoting Inspired Lives."

This book and all other Destiny Image, Revival Press, MercyPlace, Fresh Bread, Destiny Image Fiction, and Treasure House books are available at Christian bookstores and distributors worldwide.

For a U.S. bookstore nearest you, call 1-800-722-6774.

For more information on foreign distributors, call 717-532-3040.

Reach us on the Internet: www.destinyimage.com.

ISBN 13 TP: 978-0-7684-4246-5

ISBN 13 Ebook: 978-0-7684-8459-5

For Worldwide Distribution, Printed in the U.S.A.

1 2 3 4 5 6 7 8 / 18 17 16 15 14

Contents

Foreword

Procrastination is an enemy of the soul. Yesterday is gone; tomorrow is not promised. The question you must ask yourself is: "What will you do with your *now?*"

Dr. Teresa Hairston is a successful visionary. She is a woman who had a plan; worked her plan and became very successful. She now shares ten foundational principles in this awesome book, *Stop Waiting…Start Winning! 10 Essential Principles for Success.*

Biblical wisdom teaches us: "Where there is no *vision,* the people perish…" (Prov. 29:18 KJV) However, *with* vision and *with* a plan, we can escape from mediocrity and myopic thinking and escalate our lives to the great horizons of success that God has planned for us.

Dr. T. has the ability to take you there. In the Kingdom, she is known as a "Power Woman"—she leads by example.

Follow the pattern that she outlines in this book and you will grab hold of valuable tools that will help guide you to success. Jesus said, "If the blind lead the blind, *both shall fall* into the ditch" (Matt. 15:14 KJV). I truly believe that this book will guide you through the "blind spots" of life's adversities and transitions into a place of maximum impact and effectiveness!

Dr. T. will show you how to maximize your potential, develop your unexposed ability, and access your untapped strength. She will show you what you can do that you haven't done yet. She will help you go where you haven't been yet! She will provoke you to imagine what you haven't imagined yet. Get ready to soar!

I'm proud of my spiritual daughter, Dr. T! I encourage you to start reading *Stop Waiting…Start Winning!*

Bishop Paul S. Morton
Presiding Bishop, Full Gospel International Fellowship
Pastor, Changing a Generation Church, Atlanta, GA

Preface

Your vision is a "glimpse of God's glory," a distinct puzzle piece searching for placement in the big picture of God's plan. —Teresa Hairston

The most pathetic person in the world is someone who has sight but no vision. —Helen Keller

Vision Is...A Glimpse of God's Glory

One evening during the late '70s, I attended what I thought was just a gathering of friends, but turned out to be an Amway presentation. Amway became one of the world's most popular and prosperous multilevel marketing enterprises. Many Amway distributors who worked at building distribution networks to sell the company's home-cleaning products became millionaires.

Amway meetings were like pep rallies—high energy, positive, and upbeat. The facilitator motivated everyone to dream big! He'd say, "Think about what it would be like not to have any bills! How would you spend your money?" "What would you do if you had all the money you wanted and no longer had to work? How would you spend your time?"

One question which really piqued my interest that night was, "If you died tomorrow (God forbid!), what legacy would you want to leave behind?"

I pondered that question for several minutes as the facilitator went around the room soliciting answers. When it came my turn, I said, "I want to leave some type of written legacy that will positively impact others."

I didn't realize it at the time, but what the facilitator got me to do—probably for the first time in my life—was to focus on my very blurry vision and put it into words. It was a pivotal moment, a turning point in my life. In Psalm 139:13-16, David writes about how God created us:

> *You made all the delicate, inner parts of my body and knit me together in my mother's womb. Thank you for making me so wonderfully complex! Your workmanship is marvelous—how well I know it. You watched me as I was being formed in utter seclusion, as I was woven together in the dark of the womb. You saw me before I was born. Every day of my life was recorded in your book. Every moment was laid out before a single day had passed.* (NLT)

God invested a "glimpse" of His glory (an authentic and unique vision) inside you when he created you (see Jer. 1:5). A *glimpse* is "a fleeting… look"[1]; *glory* is the full manifestation or weight of a person or thing.

God created us in the spirit realm and then released us into the natural realm. God is so amazing that He ordained (ordered) each of us to be born at just the right time in history so that as we mature in and by faith, His glory is revealed or unveiled.

When we come into unity with God, His "glimpse" of glory within us is activated, and through the nurturing of the Holy Spirit, the glimpse continues to manifest into a phenomenally beautiful vision that glorifies God and edifies creation. *Vision* comes from God; it is our responsibility and opportunity to nurture and develop it. *It's up to you!*

Vision Is…A Mental Picture of Destiny

Vision is the most powerful, life-changing force that you will ever encounter in this life. Once you fully grasp it, you'll never let go of it; and it will never let you go.

Vision is *a quantifiable, qualifiable, mental picture of destiny.* It guides, drives, focuses, and motivates you through the journey of life. Without it, you meander aimlessly, subject to whims, fads, and trends. With it, your path to destiny becomes clear, creative strategies emerge, and you are able to define (or redefine) and achieve success.

Vision overcomes confusion and overwhelms complacency. A clear vision inspires you to keep moving toward your goals—no matter how many obstacles you face.

Vision is demanding, specific, and strategic. It will demand that you use every skill and talent you have. It will provide specific solutions to specific problems. It will provide timely, critical answers where beforehand, there were voids of understanding.

Introduction

Vision Dynamics and Development: A Biblical Model

Without an authentic vision, a society, business, organization, or person drifts along in ignorance; directionless. Without vision, there can be no success.

The Book of Proverbs explains: "Where there is no vision, the people perish…" (Prov. 29:18 KJV). In this context, *perish* doesn't mean to physically die, it means to "live without restraint" or "wander without purpose." The verse continues: "…but he that keepeth the law, happy is he." That word *happy* means "blessed."[1] To live according to God's vision is to live in a state of blessedness and contentment.

> **Authentic vision involves a collaboration of spiritual perspectives: retrospection, introspection, and perception.**

Retrospection (hindsight) emphasizes the value of experience and evidence. Billy Wilder, director and producer of many Oscar-winning films quipped, "Hindsight is always twenty-twenty."[2] Hindsight learns from the past—whether the result was success or failure, and applies it to current and future situations. If you've ever thought, "If I knew then what I know now…"—you're not alone! Your past has molded and shaped you for your future.

Power Quote:

Success is not final, failure is not fatal: it is the courage to continue that counts. —Winston Churchill[3]

Introspection (insight) emphasizes the capacity to discern or see into the true nature of a situation or person. Insight involves depth perception—seeing past the surface. The ancient Greeks equated insight with the "mind's eye" rather than physical eyes. They theorized that having keen insight meant having the ability to look at a situation or person (including oneself), seeing beyond outward appearances or expressions. It meant understanding and separating the components that comprise the whole. Insight is an important quality for every visionary; it reveals internal dynamics, and results in analysis, understanding, and wisdom.

Perception (foresight) emphasizes future possibilities. It looks past what is and sees what can be. Foresight is revelation of the future accompanied by a strategy. It generally makes visionaries impatient.

Foresight enables you to see the road ahead, distinguish the destination in the distance, and have a mental road map of how to get there. Others around you don't see what you see; they ask questions and request a physical map. This can be frustrating! Foresight requires great patience, care, and responsibility.

Hindsight matures; insight clarifies; and foresight guides. To be successful in your vision, you must incorporate all three.

The Vision Continuum

A continuum is a sequence or progression that evolves seamlessly. Vision develops as a continuum. Here is how it evolves:

1. *Dark.* In this stage you are not totally certain of or committed to any one path in life. You are on a quest for knowledge and understanding. You are also managing various aspects of your education, career, and intimate relationships. You find yourself "trying to make sense of it all." You have vague, intermittent flashes of awareness that there's more for you to do; but like a dream, it's fuzzy. As a result, you focus on other pursuits—career, education, personal endeavors.

2. *Hazy.* In this stage you lack clarity and certainty regarding your vision; but you are aware that you aren't where you "should" be. You have become preoccupied with "finding" your "place," so you examine past and current relationships and experiences; you contemplate your skills, talents, and present circumstances. You progressively "add things up" to try to understand why you are where you are and what is next. *But things don't add up!* You know you have to move. But where? How? You have a growing desire (and frustration) to understand and pursue *your* specific and unique vision.

3. *Clear.* In this stage you recognize and accept the fact that you have a specific vision. You are challenged as to how to reorder and manage your life circumstances and priorities in order to actively pursue what you see as "your" vision without jeopardizing the financial and physical stability of your life. Your passion to pursue your vision is now an urgent matter. You've *got* to move forward!

4. *Vivid.* In this stage your vision is clear and you are walking forward in it. You have both spoken and written it, and you are implementing your vision plan. You have made (and continue to make) the necessary sacrifices and investments—personally and professionally—to continue to grow your vision. As you continue to evolve in your vision, others see the value and viability of it. They are drawn to it, and even assigned to it. You are now challenged and stretched to embrace greater dimensions (demographically, geographically, and philosophically) for your vision, which you understand, without question, is God's way of stretching your faith. With increasing wisdom, faith, and trust in God, you and others are now running with the vision—and it's truly amazing!

Where are you on the Vision Continuum? It is important that you assess where you are in relation to your personal journey.

The Vision Model

The Bible is a book full of timeless principles and effective patterns for living. The ultimate Vision Model is presented in a small book located near the end of the Old Testament that bears the name of the prophet Habakkuk. Little is known about the life of this prophet, but this brief book focuses on the period around 600 BC, when the southern Jewish kingdom (Judah) was enduring one of the most chaotic periods in its history.

During that time, Habakkuk, one of the nation's prophets, saw the unholy lifestyles God's people were living. They were worshipping idols, their leaders were corrupt, and the entire society was in spiritual and moral decay.

Habakkuk was perplexed—not with the people, but with God. He complained to God, saying, "Why are You silent in the midst of all this chaos and wickedness?" He prayed, "God, do something!" (See Habakkuk 1:2-4.) God responded. However, His answer, which was given by way of a vision, revealed that God was going to allow an evil nation (the Chaldeans) to attack the Jews, His chosen people (see Hab. 1:5-11).

The vision wasn't what Habakkuk expected. In fact, he was so burdened by the vision that he did something no other prophet had ever done: instead of warning the people about the impending judgment of God, he went to God on *behalf* of the people: "God! Why would You allow this fierce enemy army to ravage Your beloved Jewish nation?" (See Habakkuk 1:12-17.)

After this second complaint, God gave him a second vision in Habakkuk 2:1-4; it provides a framework for how each of us should handle vision:

1. Watch for it.

I will stand my watch and set myself on the rampart, and watch to see what He will say to me, and what I will answer when I am corrected (Habakkuk 2:1 NKJV).

2. Write it down.

Then the Lord answered me and said: "Write the vision and make it plain on tablets, that he may run who reads it" (Habakkuk 2:2 NKJV).

3. Wait expectantly and patiently for it to manifest.

For the vision is yet for an appointed time; but at the end it will speak, and it will not lie. Though it tarries, wait for it; because it will surely come, it will not tarry (Habakkuk 2:3 NKJV).

4. Walk it out with humility and faith.

Behold the proud, his soul is not upright in him; but the just shall live by his faith (Habakkuk 2:4 NKJV).

Habakkuk offers great principles regarding vision.

The name *Habakkuk* (from the Hebrew word *châbaq*) means to "embrace."[4] Habakkuk first teaches us that when you embrace God's vision (no matter how outlandish it seems) your life will have impact beyond your wildest dreams!

Second, Habakkuk teaches us that in the midst of confusion, God's vision brings clarity and direction. God always answers and is always concerned at times when life or society is chaotic.

Finally, Habakkuk's Vision Model—*watch, write, wait, and walk*—is one of the clearest passages in the entire Bible about how to perceive, receive, and respond to vision.

As we journey together for the next several chapters, I will share with you Habakkuk's principles—unchanging foundational rules of vision that apply no matter what your stage or age.

This is my prayer: that this book would assist, challenge, and encourage you to understand and unleash *your vision*; that *your vision* would become a vivid reality; that *your vision* makes an indelible mark in the earth that can *never* be erased.

As you read this book, I hope you will be challenged, encouraged, equipped and empowered to move forward. Perhaps you've gotten stuck somewhere in life, but it's time to *Stop waiting and start winning!* Live your vision NOW!

Power Quote:

Vision is deeply personal and extremely distinct. Just as no two people have the same DNA or fingerprints; no two people have the same vision. You are one of a kind, and so is your vision.

Summary Questions

1. In what ways do your past experiences influence your vision?

2. Where are you on the Vision Continuum (i.e., dark, hazy, clear, or vivid)?

3. What single statement best describes your current understanding of your vision?

4. Have you written (or updated) your vision lately?

5. Where are you in the Vision Model (i.e., watching, writing, waiting, or walking)?

Phase One: WATCH

Positioning

"I will climb up to my watchtower."

Preparation

"I will...stand at my guardpost."

Perception

"There I will wait to see what the Lord says and how he will answer my complaint."
(Habakkuk 2:1).

CHAPTER ONE

The Principle of Positioning: Humility Positions You to See Vision

Life is full of challenges. Challenges are like coins; on the flip side of each one is a different picture. —Teresa Hairston

I will climb up to my watchtower
(Habakkuk 2:1).

Dynamic Definition:

Positioning: The placement of a person, product, or brand in a distinct posture relative to others.

One of my most challenging experiences was buying a home after I became self-employed. As I was going through the seemingly endless mortgage qualification process, I was made aware that my credit had some "issues." It wasn't a total bust, but there were things in my past that I hadn't quite handled correctly. These things resulted in blotches on my credit record that needed to be cleaned up before I could move forward in the home-buying process.

In order to get into position to purchase the home I really desired, I had to pay down some bills and settle lingering debts. It was frustrating to have to wait several extra months before I could proceed, but it was a great lesson that I never forgot: *In order to position myself for the type of purchase I desired, I had to change my credit status from average to excellent.* It was up to me!

I made several changes. I became meticulous about paying my monthly bills on time; I took proactive measures, making arrangements with creditors when necessary; and the *big thing*—I began to live within or below my means. In other words, if I couldn't afford an item (in most cases, *afford* meant "paying cash") *I didn't buy it!* I learned how to pass up clearance and sale racks. I quit buying things just because they were "good deals." Eventually my credit position changed.

The Humble Mindset: The Way Up Is Down

Many of the decisions we make (especially financial ones) betray a spirit of pride. Pride opposes humility. Pride says, "I want that—even if I can't afford it! I deserve it, and I don't care what it costs!" Humility says, "I am willing to wait or go without things that I don't really need." Pride says, "I'm going to get it—no matter what." Humility says, "I want my financial position and practices to honor God's plan, first and foremost!"

Living in humility will require you to embrace a mindset that is far different from today's culture. That mindset is: "The way up is down." The Bible puts it like this: "Humble yourselves before the Lord, and he will lift you up in honor" (James 4:10).

Humility is one of the most unique concepts in the Bible. Unlike many spiritual qualities like love, peace, and joy, God doesn't give you humility; you must choose it, just as Jesus did.

> *Though he was God, he did not think of equality with God as something to cling to. Instead, he gave up his divine privileges; he took the humble position of a slave and was born as a human being. When he appeared in human form, he humbled himself in obedience to God and died a criminal's death on a cross. Therefore, God elevated him to the place of highest honor and gave him the name above all other names, that at the name of Jesus every knee should bow, in heaven and on earth and under the earth, and every tongue confess that Jesus Christ is Lord, to the glory of God the Father* (Philippians 2:5-11).

Throughout the Bible, humility and honor have a symbiotic cause-and-effect relationship. If you humble yourself, God will honor you. (See Proverbs 29:23; Luke 14:11; James 4:10; First Peter 5:6.)

Positioning yourself to see God's phenomenal vision means choosing to humble yourself. "Those who exalt themselves will be humbled, and those who humble themselves will be exalted" (Matt. 23:12).

Hallmarks of Humility

From a Biblical perspective, *humility* means "modesty…lowliness of mind."[1] The greatest achievement of anyone's life is to master humility. Here is the posture of humility:

1. *Humility looks up to God as the ultimate source of power, success, and vision.* "Remember the Lord your God. He is the one who gives you power to be successful, in order to fulfill the covenant he confirmed to your ancestors with an oath" (Deut. 8:18).

2. *Humility looks up to God in the posture of perpetual thankfulness, realizing that God's grace, not talent or ability, is the catalyst for success.* "This is what the Lord says: 'Don't let the wise boast in their wisdom, or the powerful boast in their power, or the rich boast in their riches. But those who wish to boast should boast in this alone: that they truly know me and understand that I am the Lord who demonstrates unfailing love and who brings justice and righteousness to the earth, and that I delight in these things. I, the Lord, have spoken!'" (Jer. 9:23-24).

3. *Humility actively seeks ways to promote others; it is unselfish. It prefers others and focuses on legacy and future.* "Don't be selfish; don't try to impress others. Be humble, thinking of others as better than yourselves. Don't look out only for your own interests, but take an interest in others, too. (Phil. 2:3-4). "Good people leave an inheritance to their grandchildren, but the sinner's wealth passes to the godly" (Prov. 13:22).

4. *Humility exhibits love—for God first, followed by healthy self-love and love for others.* "Jesus replied, '"You must love the Lord your God with all your heart, all your soul, and all your mind." This is the first and greatest commandment. A second is equally important: "Love your neighbor as yourself."'" (Matt. 22:37-39).

Power Quote:

A leader will find it difficult to articulate a coherent vision unless it expresses his core values, his basic identity. One must first embark on the formidable journey of self-discovery in order to create a vision with authentic soul. —Mihaly Csikszentmihalyi[2]

Correctly positioning yourself to perceive and pursue God's vision for your life means deliberately embracing humility.

Habakkuk's statement, "I will *climb up to my watchtower and stand at my guardpost...*" (Hab. 2:1) indicates an intentionality about the prophet's specific spiritual positioning. Habakkuk moved from a place of darkness to a place where he could "see" what God had to show him. Notice he says *my* watchtower and *my* guardpost.

Successfully seeing God's vision depends heavily upon your individual spiritual condition which, in turn, will impact your emotional and physical relationships. In other words, pride keeps you in a position of darkness and humility elevates you to a place where you "see" the light.

Humility Repositions You

At a point in my life, I was struggling with several decisions, and in many areas, I was making bad decisions. Finally, in desperation I prayed, "God! Show ME!" What He showed me was very difficult to look at. He revealed that I was prideful and arrogant. If I was going to please God, I had to change my position and humble myself.

There are times in life when you must intentionally *move* away from your former position to a place where God can reveal Himself to you in a deeper way so you can see that "glimpse of glory." James 4:8 instructs: "Come close to God, and God will come close to you. Wash your hands, you sinners; purify your hearts, for your loyalty is divided between God and the world."

Here's how to *come close:*

1. *Daily devotion.* Prayer, Scripture reading, and meditation each morning will counteract the negative impact of the world and bring clarity regarding God's purpose for your life. In Psalm 5:3, David prays: "Each morning I bring my requests to you and wait expectantly."

2. *Memorize Scripture.* The Word of God transforms the way you think, talk, and act. It will encourage your heart to stay in a place of purity, submission, and repentance. "I have hidden your word in my heart, that I might not sin against you" (Ps. 119:11).

3. *Pray consistently.* When He walked the earth, prayer was essential to Jesus' relationship with His Father in Heaven. It is essential to ours as well. Prayer is a powerful weapon in the arsenal of a successful visionary. Prayers from the heart of a submitted servant *will* reach the heart of God. In Luke 18:1, Jesus said, "…men ought always to pray, and not to faint…" (KJV).

Humility's Prayer Life

Below are scriptures about various types of prayer. They are just a beginning point. Take time to do an in-depth study of prayer and then be intentional about developing a strong prayer life!

1. Pray biblical prayers.

    • Prayer of Faith: Pray in accordance with God's revealed or written Word and believe by faith that what you are asking from God will be done. In Mark 11:24, Jesus said, "I tell you, you can pray for anything, and if you believe that you've received it, it will be yours."

    • Prayer of Agreement: Pray with another believer who sincerely agrees with you on the goal of your prayer. In Matthew 18:19, Jesus said: "I also tell you this: If two of you agree here on earth concerning anything you ask, my Father in heaven will do it for you."

- Prayer of Consecration and Dedication: Resubmit, re-dedicate, and reconfirm your devotion to God—mind, body, soul, and strength. Reaffirm to God that your heart is humble, obedient, and willing to do whatever He instructs, especially when you are facing tough decisions and transitions. Luke 22:41-42 reads: "He walked away, about a stone's throw, and knelt down and prayed, 'Father, if you are willing, please take this cup of suffering away from me. Yet I want your will to be done, not mine.'"

- Prayer of Thanksgiving and Worship: Offer thanks to God; affirm and acknowledge His character. Start and end each day thanking and worshipping Him; no matter what circumstances look like. Praise Him in the midst of your challenges. This silences the enemy and builds your faith. "Always be joyful. Never stop praying. Be thankful in all circumstances, for this is God's will for you who belong to Christ Jesus" (1 Thess. 5:16-18). "Even though the fig trees have no blossoms, and there are no grapes on the vines; even though the olive crop fails, and the fields lie empty and barren; even though the flocks die in the fields, and the cattle barns are empty, yet I will rejoice in the Lord! I will be joyful in the God of my salvation" (Hab. 3:17-18).

- Prayer of Intercession: Pray for others. In John 17:9, Jesus prayed for His disciples: "I pray for them. I am not praying for the world, but for those you have given me, for they are yours" (NIV).

- Prayer of Binding and Loosing: This prayer encompasses several powerful principles taught by Jesus. First, as a believer, you have authority on Earth by virtue of your covenant rights through your Savior, Jesus Christ. Second, your spiritual authority to bind and loose starts on Earth because of your heavenly status as a joint-heir with Jesus Christ. And, finally, you have power because of your proper (biblically-aligned) usage of the Word of God. In Matthew 18:18-19, Jesus said: "Assuredly, I say to you, whatever you bind on earth will be bound in heaven, and whatever you loose on earth will be loosed in heaven. Again I say to you that if two of you agree on earth concerning anything that they ask, it will be done for them by My Father in heaven" (NKJV).

2. Sing. Singing songs of praise humbles and prepares your heart for God's presence. In Psalm 68:4, David declared: "Sing praises to God and to his name! Sing loud praises to him who rides the clouds. His name is the Lord—rejoice in his presence!"

3. Add fasting to your prayers. Fasting adds power to your prayers and eliminates distractions. It is a spiritual discipline that signals mature faith and intensifies results. In Matthew's Gospel, the disciples failed to cast a demonic spirit out of a young boy, but Jesus succeeded. Later, the disciples asked Jesus why they were unsuccessful. Jesus responded, "…this kind does not go out except by prayer and fasting." (Matt. 17:21 NKJV).

Your humility will position you to clearly "see" God's vision for your life without error. "God opposes the proud but favors the humble" (James 4:6).

Here are some benefits of humility:

- Humility produces agreement with God.

- Humility promotes thankfulness to God.

- Humility prepares you to receive divine vision from God.

- Humility produces spiritual peace, power, and prosperity.

"For I know the plans I have for you," declares the Lord, "plans to prosper you and not to harm you, plans to give you hope and a future" (Jeremiah 29:11 NIV).

A Time of Prayer

Right now, I need to interrupt your reading and urge you to STOP WAITING! Stop making excuses! Stop acting like you've got it together! Humble yourself today! If you do, you will change your faith position and activate a deeper dimension of God's grace! Submit yourself to God now. Reposition yourself for His perspective.

Please pray this prayer with me:

Dear heavenly Father, I humbly thank You for choosing to use me. Thank you for causing all things in my life to work together. Thank you for my specific assignment. Thank you that You love me with a perfect, unfailing, unchanging love. I will humble myself to allow your Holy Spirit to make me victorious in this vision. In the name of Jesus I pray. Amen.

But thank God! He has made us his captives and continues to lead us along in Christ's triumphal procession. Now he uses us to spread the knowledge of Christ everywhere, like a sweet perfume (2 Corinthians 2:14).

Summary Questions

1. List various *before* and *after* experiences that exemplify how you've let go of a prideful spirit and humbled yourself.

2. What patterns and habits do you currently need to change in order to grow more fully in the area of humility?

3. What patterns and habits do you currently practice that foster your growth in knowing God and understanding His Word?

4. Describe your prayer life. What types of prayer are you consistently engaged in? Take time over the next 30 days to pray all the types of prayers—do this and record God's answers!

5. Challenge yourself to add fasting to your prayer regimen. Schedule it, follow through, and then write about it.

CHAPTER TWO

The Principle of Preparation: God's Wisdom Sharpens Your Vision

Each class in the school of life teaches powerful lessons. Attentive students graduate; inattentive students repeat.—Teresa Hairston

I will…stand at my guardpost.
(Hab. 2:1).

Dynamic Definition:

Preparation: "The action or process of making something ready for use or service or of getting ready for some occasion, test, or duty."[1]

When a young person decides to enlist in the army, he or she must first attend "boot camp" and be trained for battle. One of the most shocking transitions is adjusting to the drill sergeant.

The trainee must give full attention to each and every command given by the drill sergeant or face severe discipline.

Imagine a nesting adult female bald eagle near the top of a tall pine tree located 200 yards from the lakeshore. The eagle intently watches the water. Suddenly she leaves the nest, and after a few strokes of her powerful wings, is over the water. She swoops down, snatches a fish from just below the surface with her talons and then returns to the nest to consume her prey.

Such an event would not be possible were it not for the bald eagle's remarkable eyesight. Sight is an eagle's most important sense. Scientists believe that an eagle's vision is as much as six times sharper than a human's even though the eyes are approximately the same size.[2]

Watching for your vision demands standing at attention and listening to each and every word God "speaks"; it also demands having "eagle eyes," to "see" what God shows you. God's wisdom sharpens your hearing and eyesight and will enable you to supernaturally perceive things that others around you cannot hear or see.

The Hebrew word for *watch* used by Habakkuk means "to lean forward, i.e. to peer into the distance."[3] It is not a passive act; it's an aggressive act of seeking God's wisdom. Watching for your vision means straining to perceive the vision as God gave it. In this posture you are concerned with accuracy and razor-sharp focus; your gaze is concentrated and penetrating. You don't want to grab hold of the wrong thing or the "next best" thing, so you pay attention to detail and refuse to be distracted.

Power Quote:

Wisdom is the power to see, and the inclination to choose, the best and highest goal, together with the surest means of attaining it. Wisdom is, in fact, the practical side of moral goodness. As such, it is found in its fullness only in God. He alone is naturally and entirely and invariably wise.[4]

Wisdom Triumphs over Good Advice!

Each and every day, from the time you awaken until you go to sleep, your senses are inundated with sounds, smells, tastes, and touches. It's easy to become overwhelmed to the point of sensory overload. Have you ever tried to get through a day without television, radio, Internet, or cell phones?

Life can be extremely noisy and distracting with seldom, if any, quiet time. In today's world of "talking" technology, the noise of normal life can easily distract you from clearly discerning God's vision above the voices that echo the world's point of view on every aspect of life.

And, because "faith comes by hearing" (Rom. 10:17 NKJV), when you consistently take in these viewpoints through your "ear sensors," this bombardment eventually influences your beliefs. In turn, your thoughts, plans, and goals are impacted.

Your mind is literally being filled and fed daily with information and inspiration through your ears and eyes. What have you chosen to fill yourself with?

Two Types of Wisdom

God's wisdom sharpens your gaze; so that the vision you see is clear and correct. Satan will try to distract you from seeing God's vision. He will attempt to show you a counterfeit—the wisdom of men. The Bible points out that there are two kinds of wisdom:

1. *Wisdom of men.* Paul summed this up as foolishness. Many television celebrities give "good" advice; but only godly wisdom will put you on the pathway to godly success! "Choose my instruction rather than silver, and knowledge rather than pure gold. For wisdom is far more valuable than rubies. Nothing you desire can compare with it (see Prov. 8:10-11). Good ideas and good advice are situational, circumstantial, and limited. They will fail you; but God's ideas and godly wisdom are eternal; they will transform and sustain you through every season of your life.

2. *Wisdom of God.* Paul described this as superior or divine: "Yet when I am among mature believers, I do speak with words of wisdom, but not the kind of wisdom that belongs to this world or to the rulers of this world, who are soon forgotten. No, the wisdom we speak of is the mystery of God—his plan that was previously hidden, even though he made it for our ultimate glory before the world began" (1 Cor. 2:6-7). The prophet Isaiah wrote: "'My thoughts are nothing like your thoughts,' says the Lord. 'And my ways are far beyond anything you could imagine. For just as the heavens are higher than the earth, so my ways are higher than your ways and my thoughts higher than your thoughts'" (Isa. 55:8-9).

Wisdom Triumphs over Knowledge!

Over the last 20 years, monumental technological and computer advances have changed how the entire world lives, learns, and communicates. In the 1980s, we thought fax machines were amazing; now they're all but obsolete. Today, we communicate across continents in seconds!

The worldwide web provides access to vast amounts of knowledge and information; but knowledge is not the key to success! The Bible teaches that wisdom trumps knowledge. Wisdom provides understanding as to how to apply knowledge. We may have knowledge, but without wisdom, we will have poor judgment and make bad decisions.

In the book of Proverbs, King Solomon personifies wisdom using pronouns *she* and *her:*

> *Get wisdom; develop good judgment. Don't forget my words or turn away from them. Don't turn your back on wisdom, for she will protect you. Love her, and she will guard you. Getting wisdom is the wisest thing you can do! And whatever else you do, develop good judgment. If you prize wisdom, she will make you great. Embrace her, and she will honor you. She will place a lovely wreath on your head; she will present you with a beautiful crown* (Proverbs 4:5-9).

In the Beginning…Wisdom

Many scholars have interpreted the narrative of the original sin in Genesis chapters 2 and 3, as a lesson about the dangers of disobedience, but there is another lesson: the devastating effects of rejecting God's wisdom.

> *Then the Lord God planted a garden in Eden in the east, and there he placed the man he had made. The Lord God made all sorts of trees grow up from the ground—trees that were beautiful and that produced delicious fruit. In the middle of the garden he placed the tree of life and the tree of the knowledge of good and evil* (Genesis 2:8-9).

> *The Lord God placed the man in the Garden of Eden to tend and watch over it. But the Lord God warned him, "You may freely eat the fruit of every tree in the garden—except the tree of the knowledge of good and evil. If you eat its fruit, you are sure to die"* (Genesis 2:15-17).

The serpent was the shrewdest of all the wild animals the Lord God had made. One day he asked the woman, "Did God really say you must not eat the fruit from any of the trees in the garden?" "Of course we may eat fruit from the trees in the garden," the woman replied. "It's only the fruit from the tree in the middle of the garden that we are not allowed to eat. God said, 'You must not eat it or even touch it; if you do, you will die.'" "You won't die!" the serpent replied to the woman. "God knows that your eyes will be opened as soon as you eat it, and you will be like God, knowing both good and evil." The woman was convinced. She saw that the tree was beautiful and its fruit looked delicious, and she wanted the wisdom it would give her. So she took some of the fruit and ate it. Then she gave some to her husband, who was with her, and he ate it, too (Genesis 3:1-6).

Adam and Eve rejected God's wisdom. God had given them everything they needed. But instead of focusing on the completeness of God's provision and living out the vision God had assigned them (to tend and watch over The Garden), Eve *listened* to what Satan said, and she *looked* at what Satan showed her. In verse 5 Satan says, "God knows that your eyes will be opened as soon as you eat [the forbidden fruit], and you will be like God, knowing both good and evil."

Satan distracted Eve through her ears and eyes. Eve was tricked into basing her thoughts, words and actions on what she heard and saw, rather than trusting the infinite wisdom of God. Satan was deceptively soliciting her to join him in rebellion and simultaneously forfeit her purpose.

Satan wants to destroy your future—and he is relentless! He'll say and do anything; there are no boundaries. You're never saved, sanctified, or experienced enough. He comes at you with strategic tenacity. One of his favorite tactics is to distract you through your senses.

God wanted Adam and Eve to enjoy paradise! He had made eternal provision for them, and because they were both tricked, they fell, and they forfeited God's perfect plan!

God's wisdom instructing them not to eat of the tree was actually protecting Adam and Eve; but Satan convinced Eve that God was keeping something from her. Once Eve lost focus on God's wisdom (His Word), she was open to the enemy's deception. The result was disobedience, sin, and humiliation.

If the enemy can distract you, he can destroy you. Focus on these important principles regarding God's wisdom:

- God's wisdom is the ultimate form of His love.

- God's wisdom is inerrant and complete.

- God's wisdom is all-sufficient.

- God's wisdom offers protection for His people.

- God's wisdom provides guidance.

If you want to see God's vision clearly, seek God's wisdom. Wisdom will instruct you as to how to apply knowledge.

Wisdom Triumphs over Fear!

Fear will poison your future. It is one of the most deadly weapons Satan uses against believers. He often uses fear to deceive us and try to convince us that we lack what we need to be successful in the vision God has assigned. However, "God has not given us a spirit of fear and timidity, but of power, love, and self-discipline" (2 Tim. 1:7).

Do you have fear in your heart? What are you afraid of? In an article entitled "Top 10 Strong Human Fears."[5] People ranked their top ten fears (listed from least to greatest):

10. Losing Your Freedom

9. The Unknown

8. Pain

7. Disappointment

6. Misery

5. Loneliness

4. Ridicule

3. Rejection

2. Death

1. Failure

Fear of failure is the greatest fear most people face! The only antidote for fear—is the Word of God!

And as we live in God, our love grows more perfect. So we will not be afraid on the day of judgment, but we can face him with confidence because we live like Jesus here in this world. Such love has no fear, because perfect love expels all fear. If we are afraid, it is for fear of punishment, and this shows that we have not fully experienced his perfect love (1 John 4:17-18).

Power Quote:

The greatest danger for most of us is not that our aim is too high and we miss it, but that it is too low and we reach it. —Michelangelo[6]

Wisdom Provides Clarity

A few years ago, I was in a romantic relationship with a man that I hoped to marry. He was a great guy and had all the right assets—spiritually and physically! I was very excited about the relationship and the potential. I just *knew* God had sent this man into my life, but my heart had been betrayed before and the result was brokenness. So I went to God and prayed. I asked Him to confirm to me that this was my husband.

God emphatically answered, *"No!"* But I didn't want that answer. The truth was, I was afraid that I would *never* get married! Out of fear I rejected God's wisdom and I kept moving forward with the relationship.

Months passed, and the man kept doing things to let me know that he "wasn't that into me." It was clear that the relationship was going in the wrong direction, but instead of receiving what was happening as the manifestation of God's will in my life, I continued fighting it. I kept trying to hang in there and "fix" the relationship.

Years passed. Finally, it became abundantly clear that God's answer was not only firm; it was in my best interest! He was so concerned about me and loved me so much that His mercy protected me from what was certain to become an episode of disastrous heartbreak, and a demonic attempt to derail my destiny. I had a snapshot, but God had the big picture.

As I continued to pray and get closer to God through His Word, I began to see His perspective, and my fears disappeared.

Don't worry about anything; instead, pray about everything. Tell God what you need, and thank him for all he has done. Then you will experience God's peace, which exceeds anything we can understand. His peace will guard your hearts and minds as you live in Christ Jesus (Philippians 4:6-7).

A Time of Prayer

God, I am so grateful for Your love and Your protection. There is a blessing in my obedience to You and there is safety in Your arms. Holy Spirit, please guide me into all truth and give me daily wisdom on how to handle God's truth. Today, Father, I pray for mental clarity to receive and understand Your instructions, spiritual courage to obey Your instructions without compromising or hesitating, and physical and emotional strength to consistently carry out Your instructions. In Jesus' name I pray. Amen.

Summary Questions:

1. Are you aggressively seeking God's wisdom, straining to see it as He gave it? How might your focus become more razor-sharp?

2. When you face tough decisions which is more likely to prevail in your life: the wisdom of God or of man?

3. Do your daily choices have faith in God's love and power? What distractions does Satan offer you?

4. What specific fears do you struggle with? Take time now to search for the antidote in Scripture!

CHAPTER THREE

The Principle of Perspective: Mature Faith Produces Divine Perspective of Vision

Your life is a carefully woven tapestry; an exquisite masterpiece made up of many colorful and valuable threads. —*Teresa Hairston*

There I will wait to see what the Lord says and how he will answer my complaint (Habakkuk 2:1).

Dynamic Definition:

Perspective: "A visual or mental view, as of a scene or a subject and the interrelationships of its parts or facts...."[1] "A mental outlook over time."

Several years ago, during a visit to Egypt, I toured a small rug factory on the outskirts of Cairo. The place was filled with children (supervised by a few adults) who skillfully operated looms. There were two main manufacturing rooms in the small building. The first contained several looms being operated at a frenzied pace; the second was smaller, and although there was a flurry of activity, it was apparent that these kids were older and more experienced. They used their hands and feet with rhythmic precision.

I looked at one of the rugs from the back area and remarked, "Wow! This rug is beautiful!" My tour guide quickly corrected me. "No Madame, this is not a rug, it is an exquisite tapestry."

Well. OK!

I had never seen a tapestry before. I learned that a tapestry is an intricately woven textile that is rarely laid on a floor, but is mostly hung as a piece of art. Dating back for centuries, tapestries have been woven with threads of varying quality—normally linen or cotton, but sometimes even silk, silver, or gold threads are used. Because of their delicate construction, tapestries are often very expensive or even priceless heirlooms; they can cost a few hundred, several thousands, or in some cases, millions of dollars!

The weaving process of a tapestry is interesting and instructive. Without being too technical, the process starts with two distinct sets of threads. The loom holds the first set vertically and tightly, creating the *warp*. The second set of threads is then interlaced horizontally between the first set by a device called a pick. Row by row, the pick feeds the second set of threads horizontally between the vertical threads, forming the *weft* or *weave*. The third and final step, called "beating-up or battening"—pushes the new row down against the old one. This third step is essential because it tightens the weave of the tapestry so that it becomes an artful masterpiece. Without battening, the fabric would be irregular and shapeless, and unable to withstand harsh temperatures or the test of time.

As I watched these more experienced operators, I noted the consistent, fluid motion of their hands and feet; it was mesmerizing! Their output was indeed unique. These exquisite tapestries were works of art, worthy of premium prices.

> *For we are God's masterpiece. He has created us anew in Christ Jesus, so we can do the good things he planned for us long ago* (Ephesians 2:10).

Mature Faith Is Like a Tapestry

In many ways, making exquisite tapestries parallels God's process of building faith in our lives. God, the "Master Weaver," interlaces experiences to form the "fabric" of our lives to make us into faith-filled men and women, prepared and refined for His use.

1. *Mature faith results in an exquisite tapestry woven from your life's experiences.* Just like the various types of threads that are strategically loomed together to create a unique, complex, beautiful, and textured picture. God takes your experiences— mistakes, victories and all—and strategically weaves them

together for His glory. "We know that God causes everything to work together for the good of those who love God and are called according to his purpose for them" (Rom. 8:28).

2. *Mature faith produces a testimony that glorifies God and edifies others.* Tapestries are exquisite and distinctive but they are also unique. Every tapestry tells its own story; the story may span several years or it may simply reveal an artist's singular point of view. The message of each tapestry determines where it is displayed and how its interpretation is applied. The tests and trials of your life were ordained for a specific time and a unique testimony. Never discount the intent of your past influences and present circumstances to assist you in your future assignment. "They have defeated him [Satan] by the blood of the Lamb and by their testimony" (Rev. 12:11).

3. *Mature faith is "custom built" for your assignment.* Tapestries have multiple uses. They can be used as blankets to provide warmth; or they can be hung and admired as art. Likewise, in the hands of God, your life is multidimensional and multifaceted. You are not limited by what you know and where you live. Your faith in God will allow Him to exponentially expand your impact! "Many are the plans in a person's heart, but it is the Lord's purpose that prevails" (Prov. 19:21 NIV).

4. *Mature faith is a priceless treasure.* Tapestries originate as simple balls of thread and after being skillfully woven the threads are transformed into valuable works of art. At first, your faith may be small and seem weak. Perhaps you don't believe you can accomplish a great vision, and you may not totally understand your specific assignment. However, as you mature in faith and fully embrace God's vision, provision, perspective, and protection, your faith will grow in His grace, guided by His Spirit, and your life will become victorious and infinitely impactful to other lives.

Because of our faith, Christ has brought us into this place of undeserved privilege where we now stand, and we confidently and joyfully look forward to sharing God's glory. We can rejoice, too, when we run into problems and trials, for we know that they help us develop endurance. And endurance develops strength of character, and character strengthens our confident hope of salvation. And this hope will not lead to disappointment. For we know how dearly God loves us, because he has given us the Holy Spirit to fill our hearts with his love (Romans 5:2-5).

The difference between a "nice rug" and an "exquisite tapestry" is the difference between a small measure of faith and mature faith in God. Up until now, you might have viewed your faith like a "nice rug"—fit only for common usage; but when your faith matures you will be miraculously transformed into an exquisite, unique work of art!

These trials will show that your faith is genuine. It is being tested as fire tests and purifies gold—though your faith is far more precious than mere gold. So when your faith remains strong through many trials, it will bring you much praise and glory and honor on the day when Jesus Christ is revealed to the whole world (1 Peter 1:7).

"...To change ourselves effectively, we first had to change our perceptions." —Stephen R. Covey[2]

Mature Faith Expands Your Perspective

Habakkuk needed to expand his perspective. In the opening chapter of his narrative, he complained to God about the situation around him:

*How long, O Lord, must I call for help? But you do not listen! "Violence is everywhere!" I cry, but you do not come to save. Must I forever **see** these evil deeds? Why must I **watch** all this misery? Wherever I **look**, I **see** destruction and violence"* (Habakkuk 1:2-3).

Notice how many references there are to "physical" sight. Habakkuk needed to expand his perspective, and perhaps it's time to expand yours as well!

Mature Faith Sharpens Your Spiritual Eyesight

With an expanded perspective, you see things differently. Look at the answer the Lord gave Habakkuk when He answered the prophet's initial complaint:

> *The Lord replied, "**Look** around at the nations; **look** and be amazed! For I am doing something in your own day, something you wouldn't believe even if someone told you about it. I am raising up the Babylonians, a cruel and violent people"* (Habakkuk 1:5-6).

Mature faith says look again; look and be amazed! Habakkuk is a man of faith and vision, yet he's focused on the situation he sees with his natural eyes. His perspective doesn't take into consideration the words of Isaiah 55:9: "For just as the heavens are higher than the earth, so my ways are higher than your ways and my thoughts higher than your thoughts."

It wasn't until Habakkuk gave up his ideas and thoughts and embraced God's perspective through the eyes of faith that he moved from darkness to destiny.

Power Quote:

The ultimate measure of a man is not where he stands in moments of comfort, but where he stands at times of challenge and controversy. —Martin Luther King, Jr.[3]

A mature faith perspective is the only way to "see" the future as God sees it. Through your natural eyes, you will only see a world filled with trouble; but through spiritual eyes, illuminated by mature faith, you will see God's perspective—hope for the future.

Immature faith says: "I'm miserable."

Mature faith says: "My misery will produce ministry."

Immature faith says: "I'm in pain."

Mature faith says: "My pain will produce purpose."

Immature faith says: "I can't see past my problems."

Mature faith says: "God's answer is just a prayer away."

Immature faith says: "I'm too disappointed to go on."

Mature faith says: "My disappointments are training me for God's destiny!"

Mature Faith Produces Insight

My grandparents were married when they were teens. Together they raised five children, built a life on meager means, and stayed united—through sickness and all sorts of catastrophes—until death. They were married over 60 years!

I was young when my grandparents died, but I'll never forget the atmosphere in their home. I loved being in that environment—full of peace, joy, and love. My grandfather had a million stories; he'd tell me silly jokes to make me laugh and tell me secrets. My grandmother was the world's greatest cook, and her kitchen was never without some tasty treat.

My grandparents were united by marriage, but their bond became stronger over the years because they learned each other intimately. They were one. One of them could finish the other's sentence; either could make decisions in the other's best interest.

Insight is "the power or act of seeing into a situation."[4] How amazing it is that God gives us the opportunity to "see into" the window of His purpose and vision! Mature faith makes it possible to properly perceive what God's vision is. Just like married people whose intimacy increases over time, the more time we spend with God the more we intimately "see" His perspective.

Mature Faith Produces Purity

Each choice and decision you make impacts your destiny. Even small, seemingly insignificant choices can change the trajectory of your life. It's vital that you get a correct perspective, so that you will make correct decisions that move you in a positive direction, toward (not away from) your destiny.

> *Anyone who builds on that foundation may use a variety of materials—gold, silver, jewels, wood, hay, or straw. But on the judgment day, fire will reveal what kind of work each builder has done. The fire will show if a person's work has any value. If the work survives, that builder will receive a reward* (1 Corinthians 3:12-14).

Divine Perspective Declaration

Lord, I am grateful that You have given me such a phenomenal vision for my life, and I confess now my commitment to move forward toward that vision. I submit myself with an open mind to see and receive Your perspective through the eyes of faith. According to Proverbs 3:5-6, I will trust in You with all my heart; I will not lean on my own understanding, but in all my ways, I will acknowledge You. Change, correct, and redirect me according to Your purpose and plan. In Jesus' name I pray. Amen.

You have tested us, O God; you have purified us like silver (Psalm 66:10).

Summary Questions

1. Is your faith perspective continually expanding, or are you in a stagnant state?

2. Do you find that you've been complaining about the personal or social conditions you see around you?

3. How do you see your life right now? How do you see the world? Are you in a dark place? Are your thoughts and words mostly "negative" or "positive"? Is your perspective "burdened" by personal, financial, emotional, educational, or physical concerns or public, social, political, and educational conditions?

4. Take time to pray about the level of your faith. Be honest! Embark on a journey of faith by increasing the time you spend reading and hearing God's words. Feast on Word-based messages that expand and increase your faith.

5. Make a new daily goal! Wake up each morning and make positive confessions over your day, your family, your finances, your purpose and your productivity!

Phase Two: WRITE

Publishing

"Then the Lord said to me, "Write my answer plainly on tablets…"

Perpetuation

"so that a runner can carry the correct message to others"
(Habakkuk 2:2).

CHAPTER FOUR

The Principle of Publishing: Writing Preserves and Proliferates Vision

*When the Creator of the universe takes time to speak to you...**write it down!** Just as in biblical days, when God's published record provided clarity for His people, today, your written record of God's revelation will provide focus for your life as well as others who will help to "carry" your vision. Writing your vision is one of the most important things you'll ever do.* —Teresa Hairston

Then the Lord said to me, "Write my answer plainly on tablets"
(Habakkuk 2:2).

When I was a child, I used to play a game we called "Telephone." All the players sat in a circle; the first player then whispered a sentence into the ear of the person on his or her right. Every player had to repeat the action, whispering the same sentence to the next player. No whisperer was allowed to repeat the message for clarity. Everyone was required to whisper whatever they thought they heard. When the last player got the message, he or she had to speak it aloud and confirm its accuracy with the first player.

The more players in the game, the more hilarious it became. Invariably, when the final player attempted to recite the original sentence; it had been severely altered!

The game of telephone proves God's point: *the best way to maintain the integrity of a message is to write or publish it.*

God is sovereign. He could have chosen word of mouth or any other method to spread His message; but He chose publishing. The Bible encapsulates thousands of years of God's words, thoughts, and actions. It is God's vision—in writing.

Today, there are many ways to receive messages— television, telephone, radio, Internet, and more—but printed words still leave the most legitimate, credible, and lasting impression. When people read a printed message, they tend to believe and remember it more than if they simply heard it verbally. That's not just my opinion; it is well documented that the "printed format takes on a more permanent (less likely to be tampered with) presentation."[1]

When God answered Habakkuk, His instruction was "Write the vision…" (Hab. 2:2 NKJV). God endorsed written communication in biblical times, and His endorsement stands today!

Power Quote:

Writing is….being able to take something whole and fiercely alive that exists inside you in some unknowable combination of thought, feeling, physicality, and spirit, and to then store it like a genie in tense, tiny black symbols on a calm white page. If the wrong reader comes across the words, they will remain just words. But for the right readers, your vision blooms off the page and is absorbed into their minds like smoke, where it will re-form, whole and alive, fully adapted to its new environment."
—Mary Gaitskill[2]

Publishing Transcribes Vision from the Spiritual Realm to the Physical Realm

Deuteronomy 31:9 says, "Moses *wrote* this law and delivered it to the priests…" (NKJV). This tradition evolved into the single most important, best-selling book ever written—the Bible which has inspired billions of people's faith for more than 3,000 years!

The Bible is God's written vision for His people; it guides, motivates, and inspires. Likewise, your written vision from God will guide, motivate, and inspire you and others.

Writing your vision provides physical clarity of God's spiritual revelation. Clarity is imperative if you and others are going to perform God's vision with precision; otherwise, you might find that you (or others) are accomplishing a "version of the vision" instead of the original.

Clarity of vision will literally save lives. Proverbs 29:18 confirms: "Where there is no vision, the people perish: but he that keepeth the law, happy is he" (KVJ). The word *perish* means "to live without restraint."

Publishing Changes Culture

The Bible provides several powerful examples of how a written vision saves lives. One of the most remarkable narratives about the importance of publishing the vision is found in Second Kings, chapters 22 and 23.

These passages focus on King Josiah, a descendant of David. Josiah became king when he was only eight years old, but he chose to serve the true and living God of Israel (see 2 Kings 22:1). At the age of 26, Josiah launched a Temple restoration project and one day, as one of the areas was being cleared to accommodate the renovation, Josiah's high priest, Hilkiah discovered a scroll.

> *Hilkiah the high priest said to Shaphan the court secretary, "I have found the Book of the Law in the Lord's Temple!" Then Hilkiah gave the scroll to Shaphan, and he read it....Shaphan also told the king, "Hilkiah the priest has given me a scroll." So Shaphan read it to the king. When the king heard what was written in the Book of the Law, he tore his clothes in despair* (2 Kings 22:8, 10-11).

Josiah had chosen to worship the one true God, where many of his predecessors had not. In fact, for 57 years before Josiah's reign, the kings of Israel were evil and worshipped idol gods; as a result, the people began to worship idols and pagan gods and were unconcerned with God's law. They were perishing spiritually, and God became angry.

The scroll Hilkiah found, which was most likely the Book of Deuteronomy, was a turning point in Josiah's life and the history of the nation. When he heard the truth of God's Word, Josiah launched a campaign to come into complete compliance with God's laws. As a result, the nation's culture changed and turned back to God.

Then the king summoned all the elders of Judah and Jerusalem. And the king went up to the Temple of the Lord with all the people of Judah and Jerusalem, along with the priests and the prophets—all the people from the least to the greatest. There the king read to them the entire Book of the Covenant that had been found in the Lord's Temple. The king took his place of authority beside the pillar and renewed the covenant in the Lord's presence. He pledged to obey the Lord by keeping all his commands, laws, and decrees with all his heart and soul. In this way, he confirmed all the terms of the covenant that were written in the scroll, and all the people pledged themselves to the covenant.

Josiah tore down the altars that the kings of Judah had built on the palace roof above the upper room of Ahaz. The king destroyed the altars that Manasseh had built in the two courtyards of the Lord's Temple. He smashed them to bits and scattered the pieces in the Kidron Valley. The king also desecrated the pagan shrines east of Jerusalem, to the south of the Mount of Corruption, where King Solomon of Israel had built shrines for Ashtoreth, the detestable goddess of the Sidonians; and for Chemosh, the detestable god of the Moabites; and for Molech, the vile god of the Ammonites. He smashed the sacred pillars and cut down the Asherah poles. Then he desecrated these places by scattering human bones over them (2 Kings 23:1-3; 12-14).

Once Josiah got the published Word, he understood and embraced the truth of God's vision for Israel. He then set out aggressively about the task of completely overhauling the culture!

Publishing Saves Lives: Esther's Example

Another example of the power of the published Word is found in the amazing Esther narrative. In the second chapter of the Book of Esther, the beautiful young Jewish woman was groomed to become the new queen to the powerful Persian king, Xerxes (see Esther 2:17).

Esther's older cousin Mordecai, who was also her guardian, wisely advised her to conceal her Jewish heritage from the King and his court (especially since the Jews were captives of the Persians). Later, Mordecai overhears two of the king's aides plotting to kill the king and sends a warning to the king through Esther. As a result, the king's life is saved and Mordecai is given credit in the royal records.

As time goes on, the king chooses an egomaniacal man named Haman to be his new prime minister, a powerful position in the kingdom. Haman's position dictated that everyone bow to him, but Mordecai refused to bow because of his devotion to God. Haman reacts violently—taking offense, and devises a plot to kill Mordecai (as well as all the Jews in the land), and subtly gets King Xerxes to approve the plan.

Mordecai learns of the plan and goes to Esther to ask her to plead with the king to intervene to save the Jews, but Esther is afraid because custom dictates that she can only go before the king if he summons her. Outside of that, she faces immediate execution for such a bold move. However, Esther courageously decides to go to the king anyway. First, she tells Mordecai to gather all the Jews for a three-day fast. Then, having resolved to approach the king she says, "…If I perish, I perish" (Esther 4:16 NKJV).

After the three-day fast, the favor of God is evident. Esther's visit to the king meets with positive results. King Xerxes extends his scepter as a gesture that he is pleased to see her. He still has no idea that she and Mordecai are Jews, or that wicked Haman's plan to kill the Jews was spawned from his hatred of Mordecai. It appears that Esther's efforts are too little and too late; however, the night before the mass execution, the king has insomnia:

> *That night the king had trouble sleeping, so he ordered an attendant to bring the book of the history of his reign so it could be read to him. In those records he discovered an account of how Mordecai had exposed the plot of Bigthana and Teresh, two of the eunuchs who guarded the door to the king's private quarters. They had plotted to assassinate King Xerxes* (Esther 6:1-2).

After reading the book of history (most likely, the Book of Chronicles), King Xerxes honors Mordecai, kills Haman, and cancels the plan to annihilate the Jews.

Publishing Gives Revelation

When writing your vision, consider the following:

1. Details make the difference. Include as much detail as possible in your vision. Write everything God shows you, no matter how far-fetched it may seem.

2. Despise not the day of small beginnings. God may reveal a small "seed" of the vision in one season and add to it in another; but rest assured, God's vision is perfect and powerful.

3. Don't be intimidated. God's power resides in His Word; it will overwhelm and overtake any system or man-made power—no matter how high or entrenched it is.

4. Dare to see through God's eyes. Things that seem like the status quo to others will be unacceptable for you; things that seem revolutionary and extreme to others will be minimal starting points for you.

5. Dare to obey in every aspect of the vision. God's revelation will define your destiny and save generations. Your vision will reform culture, change the future, and surpass your life span.

Publishing Has Infinite Impact

As you write your vision, take seriously the power of God's words.

Through faith we understand that the worlds were framed by the word of God, so that things which are seen were not made of things which do appear (Hebrews 11:3 KJV).

The Lord merely spoke, and the heavens were created. He breathed the word, and all the stars were born (Psalm 33:6).

For six days God spoke: "Let there be…" and there *was* (see Genesis 1).

- *God's words shaped the world.* Your published words will shape your world.

- *God's words shape destinies.* Your published words will shape destinies.

- *God's words shape generations.* Your published words will shape generations.

- *God's words change lives.* Your published words will change lives.

- *God's words build futures.* Your published words will build futures.

The summation of Josiah's life is a powerful legacy:

Never before had there been a king like Josiah, who turned to the Lord with all his heart and soul and strength, obeying all the laws of Moses. And there has never been a king like him since (2 Kings 23:25).

As you approach writing (publishing) your vision, expect your written vision to become the tangible representation of God's revelation in your life; and leave your "mark" in the earth—a mark that will never be erased.

A Time of Prayer

God, I thank You for the revelation of vision and the opportunity to write what You've shown me in words. I pray that You will give me wisdom to write words inspired directly by You. I realize that there is no power in my words—only in Your Word as it has been revealed to me through your Holy Spirit. According to Isaiah 55:11, Your Word always produces fruit and accomplishes everything You want it to and prospers everywhere You send it. God, please give me a deeply profound revelation of Your precise vision and the powerful words to express that vision. May the words I write be life, hope, and healing to those who hear and read them. In Jesus' name I pray. Amen.

Summary Questions

1. Have you written your vision? If not, start now! Begin by clearing your mind and schedule so you can quietly "hear" the

voice of the Holy Spirit as He speaks to you about your vision. As He does, be faithful to write everything He says, and *only* what He says.

2. If you've already written out your vision, take time to review and perhaps update it (if it's been longer than a year since you wrote or revised it).

CHAPTER FIVE

The Principle of Perpetuation: Perpetuated Truth Has Infinite Transformative Power

Perpetuating truth establishes legacy and changes culture. This will be the greatest opportunity and challenge of your life! —*Teresa Hairston*

Then the Lord said to me, "Write my answer plainly on tablets, so that a runner can carry the correct message to others" (Habakkuk 2:2).

"As a young boy, Alex Haley first learned of his African ancestor, Kunta Kinte, by listening to the family stories of his maternal grandparents while spending his summers in Henning, Tennessee."[1] Although writing came easily for Haley, his formal writing career didn't begin until he was 41, when his first successful article appeared in *Playboy Magazine*. Nine years later, in 1976, his book, *Roots,* was published.[2]

A year later, *Roots* became a landmark television miniseries that riveted America. For the first time in prime-time TV, African Americans were featured as heroes being victimized by whites. The series portrayed the atrocities of the slave trade, as well as the inhumanity of a dominant culture toward minorities, based on skin color.

Network execs wrongly predicted that *Roots* would flop. To the contrary: "*Roots* scored higher [viewership] ratings than any previous entertainment program in history."[3]

Vernon Jordan, former president of the Urban League, called it "the single most spectacular educational experience in race relations in America." Over 250 colleges and universities planned courses on the saga, and during the broadcast, over 30 cities declared "Roots" weeks.[4]

Beyond the 110 million people who saw the final episode of *Roots* were future generations that, as a result of the series, changed their views on race relations. Two other developments can also be traced to *Roots*. First, there was a marked rise in family reunions and booming cottage industry for businesses that trace ancestral lineage. Second, there was an explosion of African-American writers who began to publish books of all types.

Alex Haley's life and book changed the culture.

Truth Is Often Hard to Handle

The plain truth can be hard to handle. *Roots* was a tough pill to swallow for many Americans who had never contemplated the horrendous acts of slavery. The most memorable line in another movie, *A Few Good Men,* came from the character, Colonel Nathan Jessep, played by Jack Nicholson. While under oath and being grilled by the prosecutor, the Colonel decided to reveal the truth—that there had been a cover-up of illegal and deadly deeds. He exploded with the words: "You can't handle the truth!"

Truth exposes secrets. It can be extremely abrasive because it's often *easier* to avoid complete transparency.

When God instructed Habakkuk to record His message plainly on tablets so that any runner could carry the message correctly, God knew that the truth in the message was going to be difficult for listeners to receive and believe. Yet God always instructs us to deliver truth without compromise.

"Write my answer plainly" (Hab 2:2). The root of the Hebrew word for *plain* means "to dig" or "to engrave."[5] By engraving the vision in stone, it would not only endure, but it would be easy to interpret. The tedious engraving process also discouraged the use of unnecessary words that could clutter or compromise the message.

Anyone who publishes a book or writes an article will tell you that it is often easier to use many words than it is to handpick the few words that best convey a clear, concise message and avoid misinterpretation.

In Ephesians 3:8-10, the apostle Paul expressed the need for his God-given vision to be plainly written:

And so here I am, preaching and writing about things that are way over my head, the inexhaustible riches and generosity of Christ. My task is to bring out in the open and make plain what God, who created all this in the first place, has been doing in secret and behind the scenes all along. Through followers of Jesus like yourselves gathered in churches, this extraordinary plan of God is becoming known and talked about even among the angels! (MSG).

Jesus used stories called *parables* because He understood the critical importance of making His messages plain. He didn't deliver complicated messages that required theoretical analysis by educated scholars. Parables used common language and incorporated images that listeners could relate to; this was one of Jesus' primary methods for teaching Kingdom principles.

John 8:32 records the words of Jesus: "And you will know the truth, and the truth will set you free." Initially, the truth may be hard to handle, but eventually it will be the key to freedom from your past, your preconceived notions, and your inferior plans.

God's words of truth will lead you and others to success. Don't try to dress up your vision with your words—just say what God said and let Him be responsible for the results!

Power Quote:

The plain and simple truth of your vision will guide and govern behaviors, beliefs, values and symbols—this "culture" when repeated and replicated is foundational to the perpetuation of your vision.

Power Quote:

The very essence of leadership is [that] you have a vision. It's got to be a vision you articulate clearly and forcefully on every occasion. You can't blow an uncertain trumpet. —Theodore Hesburgh[6]

Truth Repeated Will Be Perpetuated

"Repetition increases the chance that you get heard,"[7] says entrepreneur, author and public speaker, Seth Godin. "Repetition also increases (for a while) the authority and believability of what you have to say. Listeners go from awareness of the message to understanding to trust. Yes, the step after that is annoyance, which is the risk the marketer always faces. Delivering your message in different ways, over time, not only increases retention and impact, but it gives you the chance to describe what you're doing from several angles."[8]

In today's sight-and-sound generation, we are so inundated with advertisements via television, radio, Internet, and other media formats, that we sometimes find ourselves—without even thinking about it—humming a tune that we've heard numerous times on some TV commercial. Yes! Marketers have discovered the power of repetition to reinforce a message. However, marketers didn't create the concept!

Every time you see a rainbow, you see God's covenant symbol being perpetuated through repetition.

Speaking to Noah, "God said:

This is the sign of the covenant which I make between Me and you, and every living creature that is with you, for perpetual generations: I set My rainbow in the cloud, and it shall be for the sign of the covenant between Me and the earth (Genesis 9:12-13 NKJV).

Every time you hear the Gospel, you hear the truth of God's Word being perpetuated through repetition.

Just before Jesus ascended into Heaven, He plainly gave His Great Commission to His disciples:

I have been given all authority in heaven and on earth. Therefore, go and make disciples of all the nations, baptizing them in the name of the Father and the Son and the Holy Spirit. Teach these new disciples to obey all the commands I have given you. And be sure of this: I am with you always, even to the end of the age (Matthew 28:18-20).

When Paul wrote about the sacred ordinance of Communion, he instructed: "For every time you eat this bread and drink this cup, you are announcing the Lord's death until he comes again" (1 Cor. 11:26).

Every time you participate in Communion, you are expressing your belief and perpetuating your commitment to the One True God.

Reflect on the words of your vision to make sure they are accurate and convey your exact meaning. Repeat the truth of your vision to your family, friends and coworkers. Replicate your vision in various formats—

add graphics to increase its impact. The repetition and replication of your vision will expand and increase it so that it can be carried by others.

Power Quote:

Having a Vision is not enough. It must be combined with imagination, determination, faith, hope and passion. It is not enough to just stare up at the stars...we must become the stars that the stars shine down on. —Victoria June[9]

Uncompromised Truth Propels Vision Forward

How big do *you* see your vision? Have you perceived it as big enough to impact nations and generations?

Don't make the mistake of undervaluing or underexposing your vision. The God who gave you the vision is omniscient, omnipresent, and omnipotent. Your unwavering faith in God's truth, combined with courageous action, is what will make His vision through you as big, as great, and as world changing as He allows!

God's truth has multigenerational impact! "Good people leave an inheritance to their grandchildren." (Prov. 13:22) Even the tiniest glimpse of His glory invested in you is bigger than anything you can imagine. That glimpse, when properly nurtured by faith, will extend beyond your life and lifetime.

God's truth is the propeller of vision. Everything that moves is propelled by a power source. When you ride on an airplane you experience the power of a sophisticated hydraulic-based propulsion system. This system lifts, propels and lands the plane. If there is a problem in the hydraulic system, it is a serious issue! Likewise, if you compromise God's truth as you implement your vision, it will crash and burn!

God's truth will never compromise to accommodate sin. In Habakkuk 2, God's words to the prophet were hard to handle, but they were the truth. His words contained the power to change the world. The runner's responsibility was to carry the correct message, not a convenient message that people would like.

Many people attempt to compromise God's truth to justify their individual desires or get "buy-in" from others. There's a very simplistic illustration of this compromise: Take a clean, clear glass and pour it full of water. That glass of water is pure and ready for drinking. Now, add just a teaspoon of dirt and it becomes contaminated and unfit for drinking.

It is that way with God's truth. We are commanded not to add or subtract anything from it (see Deut. 4:2; Prov. 30:6; Rev. 22:18-19).

There are times when you will want to add your own "twist" onto the vision that God has given you. You will reason with yourself about incorporating ideas to gain more funding, get more sales, attract bigger crowds, and so on. However, let me caution you: if the things you want to do are not things that God told you to do, or the timing of God, do yourself a favor—save your time, energy, and money! Do *only* what God tells you and do *all* of what God tells you; and don't do *anything* that He *doesn't* tell you!

Solomon gives valuable wisdom in Proverbs 4:20-27:

> *My child, pay attention to what I say. Listen carefully to my words. Don't lose sight of them. Let them penetrate deep into your heart, for they bring life to those who find them, and healing to their whole body. Guard your heart above all else, for it determines the course of your life. Avoid all perverse talk; stay away from corrupt speech. Look straight ahead, and fix your eyes on what lies before you. Mark out a straight path for your feet; stay on the safe path. Don't get sidetracked; keep your feet from following evil.*

Truth Contains Hope

God's vision to Habakkuk contained hope for the prophet's dismal circumstances and the nation's degradation. In fact, although Habakkuk couldn't immediately see it, God's vision provided the *only* hope for the perplexing situation.

Initially, truth may sting with pain, but it is the only path to victory.

There are times when truth causes a shift in our lives, and the turnaround causes us to think things are getting worse. Sometimes the truth of a situation shines a light on things that we would rather not see; but our total and complete trust must be in God's perfect way, and not our own plans. He has said: "'I know the plans I have for you,' says the Lord. 'They are plans for good and not for disaster, to give you a future and a hope'" (Jer. 29:11).

God's vision through Habakkuk, turned the entire nation around—and it was for the better! God knew what His people needed, and He knows what you and I need. His vision is the prescription for any and every problem; it is hope for a bright future.

God's vision contains truth, truth contains hope, and hope contains the power to propel you and others who read it forward. This allows you to run and continue to run. Generations will run when they read your vision. Nations will run when they read your vision!

The apostle Paul wrote in Romans 5:1-5:

Therefore, since we have been made right in God's sight by faith, we have peace with God because of what Jesus Christ our Lord has done for us. Because of our faith, Christ has brought us into this place of undeserved privilege where we now stand, and we confidently and joyfully look forward to sharing God's glory. We can rejoice, too, when we run into problems and trials, for we know that they help us develop endurance. And endurance develops strength of character, and character strengthens our confident hope of salvation. And this hope will not lead to disappointment. For we know how dearly God loves us, because he has given us the Holy Spirit to fill our hearts with his love.

Power Quote:

Where there is no hope in the future, there is no power in the present.
—John Maxwell[10]

A Time of Prayer

Please join me in this prayer. Better yet, take out a sheet of paper and write your own prayer in your own words. Carry it with you as you go about your day, and pull it out and read it from time to time. May the words of your prayer encourage you to trust in God and put your hope in His unwavering promises for your life.

Dear God, You've done incredible things for people who've followed Your vision for their lives. I am in awe of Your power to create strength where there has been weakness. I know that You can indeed do all things.

Father, I need Your guidance, I need You to order my steps and establish my thoughts each day. I am committed to the vision You gave me, but I need Your clarity for this next season.

So today, according to Your Word in Matthew 18:18, that says, "whatever you forbid on earth will be forbidden in heaven, and whatever you permit on earth will be permitted in heaven," I forbid fear from influencing my mind. I forbid doubt from influencing my words, I forbid any action that would detour me from the big faith steps that You order me to take. God, release Your power in my life; release Your love in my life. I declare that I have a sound mind and that Your blessings and promises are overtaking me, right now!

Right now, I embrace a new dimension of courage for my vision and I declare by Your power that this vision will be perpetuated in such a profound way, that men and women in this generation and future generations will know that this is the Lord's work and it is marvelous!

Thank You for trusting me with this vision; thank You for using me to perpetuate this vision. In Jesus' name. Amen.

Summary Questions

1. As you review your vision statement and your vision plan, is it plain enough to be understood by the average person?

2. As you review your vision statement and your vision plan, is it big enough to impact nations and generations?

3. Review your vision statement. Take time to share it with close friends and get honest feedback on whether or not it is easy to understand. (NOTE: Don't seek opinions on the content of the statement and DO NOT share your plan.)

4. As you review your vision statement and your vision plan, is it the whole truth and nothing but the truth? Have you clearly heard and recorded God's word to you? This is a critical step before moving forward.

Phases One and Two: Summary

Time to Reflect

If you've been following Habakkuk's Vision Model, you are positioned, prepared, and poised to move forward. You are now at a pivotal point in your journey. You have grown in the following ways:

- You are now functioning in a realm of true humility, godly wisdom, and mature faith.

- You realize that God could have chosen someone else, but He graciously chose you to be the solution to a specific problem in the earth.

- You have received, believed, and written God's vision for your life.

- You are positioned, spiritually, psychologically, and emotionally, to move forward and be used by God as a blessing to nations and generations.

Welcome to your new season—a season of breakthrough and breakout! As you prepare for the next steps on your journey to actualize God's promise of fulfilled vision in your life, consider the interesting aspects of the promise God gave Abram in Genesis 12:1-3:

The Lord had said to Abram, "Leave your native country, your relatives, and your father's family, and go to the land that I will show you. I will make you into a great nation. I will bless you and make you famous, and you will be a blessing to others. I will bless those who bless you and curse those who treat you with contempt. All the families on earth will be blessed through you."

God made three distinct promises to Abram:

1. The Land Promise

2. The National Promise

3. The Spiritual Promise

On your journey to fulfill vision, please understand that there will be all types of challenges and obstacles—emotional, spiritual, physical, and psychological. Following God's vision for your life does not give you immunity to problems or difficulties. In fact, it is precisely because you *are* willing to follow God's vision that the enemy has drawn an even bigger target on your back!

There is much at stake; this is a critical time to draw closer to God than ever before in your life! Study God's Word, pray over your vision, and discipline your flesh! Believe that God's covenant promises for your life are as real for you as they were for Father Abram because, through the blood of Jesus, you are Abram's descendant and a joint-heir to God's promises!

1. Your Land Promise. *You have a tangible "promised land."*

When Moses led the children of Israel out of Egyptian bondage, he was leading them toward a land of freedom. The only reason the Israelites wandered in the wilderness for 40 years (instead of taking the direct ten-day route), was because of their doubt, disobedience, and unbelief. God was faithful to His covenant promise. Yet with the exception of Joshua and Caleb—the only two who believed and did not doubt the promise—the rest of the Israelites who left Egypt missed the unparalleled joy of entering into the land "flowing with milk and honey" (Num. 13:27), where they would flourish and prosper.

Just like the land that was promised to Abram and possessed by Joshua, your land is your optimal place of productivity, abundance, and prosperity. The key to possessing your promised land is to walk in humility, wisdom, obedience, and faith toward God's promised vision—without doubting.

2. Your National Promise. *You will bless nations and generations!*

God promised Abram "I will make you into a great nation. I will bless you and make you famous, and you will be a blessing to others" (Genesis 12:2).

Because of God's promise, Abraham's lineage was extended through Isaac and Jacob and then through all the generations of the earth. All his generations were blessed—even those that came through his son, Ishmael. That means *all* his generations, including you and me!

When you study the narrative regarding Abram, you will find that he made lots of mistakes and experienced numerous setbacks. In his lifetime Abram would probably have been voted Least Likely to Have Generational Impact. But God was still faithful to His promise to Abram! When Abram (renamed *Abraham*) was 100 years of age, God allowed him and his wife Sarah to bring forth Isaac, the child of promise.

One of the things that Abraham teaches us is that God is sovereign. *God uses whom He chooses.* God chose Abraham—a man full of imperfections, flaws, and fears. Abraham did all sorts of sinful things, but God still chose him. When Abraham repented, God forgave him and restored him. Don't ever give up on your God-vision! There is nothing too hard for God! No matter what you've done in your past, or how many mistakes and setbacks you've experienced, God is faithful! He's the ultimate Promise Keeper. He chose you!

God wants to use you, and He's already blessed you so that you can bless others! He's waiting for you to transform your thinking.

When Abram transformed his thinking, he went from being Abram (exalted father) into Abraham (father of many nations), and Sarai (princess) became Sarah (mother of nations). (See Genesis 17:5,15-16). When you put your total faith and trust in God, your faith activates a miraculous transformation process that results in you becoming a better "you" than you have ever been or could ever be without Him. Stop waiting! Start winning!

> *For you are all children of God through faith in Christ Jesus. And all who have been united with Christ in baptism have put on Christ, like putting on new clothes. There is no longer Jew or Gentile, slave or free, male and female. For you are all one in Christ Jesus. And now that you belong to Christ, you are the true children of Abraham. You are his heirs, and God's promise to Abraham belongs to you* (Galatians 3:26-29).

3. Your Spiritual Promise. *You have been chosen by God.*

But you are the ones chosen by God, chosen for the high calling of priestly work, chosen to be a holy people, God's instruments to do his work and speak out for him, to tell others of the night-and-day difference he made for you (1 Peter 2:9 MSG).

God's plan for your future has not been cancelled by the mistakes of your past. From the beginning of time, man has sinned and fallen short of God's glory (glory is the full manifestation of a thing or person). Adam and Eve sinned and missed a lifetime in paradise; Abraham sinned, Moses sinned, David sinned—and you and I have sinned. Does this excuse us from pursuing God's righteousness? *Absolutely not!* But it should humble us as we embrace God's grace, His unmerited favor.

God chose you for a special assignment, and His assignment comes with the authority and ability to accomplish it! It is not limited by time or circumstances. When Abraham finally accepted his assignment, he was 100 years old; but God's assignment for Abraham's future was not cancelled by Abraham's past.

The Progressive Revelation of God's Vision

Abraham helps us to understand an important concept—*progressive revelation*. God didn't reveal the totality of His promises to Abraham in one revelation. In Genesis 12:2, God promised Abram many descendants; but it wasn't until 24 years later that God revealed to him that the child of promise would come from his union with Sarah. In Genesis 12:2, God promised Abram the land of Canaan, but it would take 400 years for the possession to manifest.

Could God have shown Abraham everything all at once? Of course! But this is how God works. In His infinite wisdom, God chooses to reveal vision. As you grow in faith, God reveals more and more vision. It's up to you—faith comes by hearing, and the "hearing" must be through the "ear" of your heart.

I pray that your hearts will be flooded with light so that you can understand the confident hope he has given to those he called—his holy people who are his rich and glorious inheritance (Ephesians 1:18).

Phase Three: WAITING

Process

"The vision is yet for an appointed time;
but at the end it will speak, and it will not lie."

Patience

"Though it tarries, wait for it; because it will surely come,
it will not tarry" (Habakkak 2:3 NKJV).

CHAPTER SIX

The Principle of Process: God's Process Yields God's Promised Vision

The processes of life, though often tedious and tasteless, are necessary to perfect us. —Teresa Hairston

The vision is yet for an appointed time; but at the end it will speak, and it will not lie.
(Habakkuk 2:3 NKJV).

Dynamic Definition:

Process: "A series of actions, changes, or functions bringing about a result...."[1]

In the winter of 2009, my brother died. It was one of the most painful experiences of my life. I couldn't believe that my brother had closed his eyes for the last time; I certainly felt pain unlike any I'd ever known.

My brother and I lived in different cities. By the time I got to him, we had only one day together in the hospital. That day was a blur of doctors, nurses, decisions, emotions, prayer, and bewilderment. I didn't even have time to call people to pray for him.

After the whole ordeal, I relived that last day, moment by moment, countless times. Always I'd think, *God! Why couldn't I have had more time? What could I have done differently? How could I have saved him?*

There were so many life-and-death decisions to make so rapidly. I didn't want to make them but I had no choice. I second-guessed myself a thousand times in the months that followed. My anger turned to helplessness and then despair. *Why me? Why now? It isn't fair!*

Finally, I let my brother go. He asked me to let him go; I had no choice. He was in pain; but so was I. I let him go…*I had to.*

Long after the funeral, my world kept spinning. It didn't stop or even slow down for a long time.

Psychologists say that when we experience a major loss, we pass through five stages of grief: denial, anger, bargaining, depression, and acceptance.

I don't know where one stage stopped and the next started, but I do know that it was a season of misery. At times I would just break down and cry uncontrollably—no matter where I was. At other times, I refused to look at photos of my brother. At still other times, I would stare at his photo for hours.

I felt like I was coming apart at the seams, yet I had to go on with my life; I couldn't quit.

Finally, a friend said, "Cry as long and as loud as you need to. It's part of the process." I did. Still, I just wanted the pain to stop and the grief to go away. I wondered, *When is this going to end?*

The lesson was humbling. In life, there are some processes that you can't control; you simply must go through them to get to the other side.

Process: The Divine Perspective

Experiencing life's difficult processes is inevitable. There are some processes in life you simply can't avoid. However, if you have a godly perspective in and through these challenges, you will find fulfillment instead of frustration and you will ultimately experience joy instead of despair.

In Second Corinthians 12, Apostle Paul wrote about the amazing vision that God showed him (see 2 Cor. 12:1-4), but he also confessed that he struggled with an infirmity throughout his ministry. Many theologians think this infirmity was malaria or a physical ailment.

Paul asked God to heal him, but God chose not to; instead of being frustrated, Paul adapted a godly perspective—he determined that his infirmity helped him realize his need to totally depend on God's power and provision.

In Second Corinthians 12:10, he wrote, "That's why I take pleasure in my weaknesses, and in the insults, hardships, persecutions, and troubles that I suffer for Christ. For when I am weak, then I am strong."

Process of Time: Chronos and Kairos

Everything in life involves a process or cycle that occurs in the context of time.

In Genesis 8:22, God said: "As long as the earth remains, there will be planting and harvest, cold and heat, summer and winter, day and night."

The ancient Greeks didn't measure time down to minutes and seconds as we do. Time was perceived in general terms, and hours varied in length.[2]

> The ancient Greeks had two words for time, chronos and kairos. [Chronos] refers to chronological or sequential time, [kairos] signifies a time between, a moment of indeterminate time in which something special happens."[3]

Man operates in chronos, or measured time; God operates in kairos—an opportune or supreme moment. The determination of when kairos moments take place is in accordance with God's sovereignty, and is far beyond our human grasp of understanding or control. However, God's timing is always perfect and our submission to His timing is critical to our personal peace.

A kairos moment is a God-given moment of destiny in which humanity has the opportunity to step forward into God's divine opening. It is the moment when the natural and the spiritual realms come together—a God-appointed moment unbounded by humanity.

Here are some examples of kairos moments: the birth of Jesus Christ; the death, burial, and resurrection of Jesus Christ (see Rom. 5:6); the day of Pentecost. The second coming of Christ will also be a kairos moment (see Mark 13:33).

The most important moment of your life will be when God opens a supernatural door and creates a kairos moment for your vision to come into fruition. You can't predict, orchestrate, or control a kairos moment or season, you can only prepare for it and anticipate it by faith. Your vision is already promised by God, and at His kairos moment, it will manifest.

Power Quote:

The person who sees the difficulties so clearly that he does not discern the possibilities cannot inspire a vision in others. —J. Oswald Sanders[4]

Process: The Overcomer Perspective

The Habakkuk narrative clearly indicates that there were points of frustration and disappointment in the life of the prophet as he waited for God's "appointed time." Likewise, there will be times in the midst of your waiting process that you will face frustration, disappointment, and even the temptation to give up. The enemy of your soul and vision wants to discourage you to the point that you stop believing in God's kairos moment for your vision to manifest.

People who have given up in the midst of difficulties, frustrations, and challenges, will not be attacked with consistently escalating levels of trials because the enemy has already won! But as a visionary with a passion to pursue the full manifestation of God's glory, the enemy's target on your back is specific and strategic. He has "custom-designed" traps for you; but remember, you already know the outcome: at the "appointed time"—your God-vision will prevail!

In the meantime, like the prophet, you must continue to move forward in the process, believing for the promise!

Your faith declarations are vital in seasons of processing when you are weathering the inevitable storms of life.

In John 10:10, Jesus exposes the enemy's plan: "The thief's purpose is to steal and kill and destroy." The words that Jesus uses here are insightful: *thief, steal, kill,* and *destroy.* These words have deep meaning and application for you as a visionary. The word *thief* comes from the Greek word *klepto,* which means to "steal."[5]

If you've ever walked down a crowded sidewalk in a metropolitan city, you've probably clutched your pocketbook closely or exercised more vigilance regarding the location of your wallet, to avoid being pickpocketed. A skilled thief can steal from you with the slightest contact; his goal is to steal your valuables without your even knowing it!

That's the way the devil works. He seeks to deceptively rob you of your vision by injecting doubt and fear into your thought life. If he can get you distracted from having total and complete faith in God's vision for your life, he can get you off the path of vision and onto the path of destruction.

The word *kill* in this passage is the Greek word *thuo,* which means to "sacrifice."[6] In this context, the thief comes to convince you to make a sacrifice of something precious—i.e. your vision!

The truth is this: The devil can't take your vision from you, because he doesn't have the power. That's why he tries to put enough stumbling blocks in your way that you fall down time after time. What he's hoping is that, at some point, you'll decide not to get back up again. But Proverbs 24:16 encourages the opposite, saying: "The godly may trip seven times, but they will get up again."

In times of stress and challenge, *never* sacrifice your vision. Even if you are moving forward at a snail's pace—keep moving! Don't put your vision down or push it aside; you never know when God's kairos moment will manifest!

Even in times of devastation—no matter what happens or how hard you fall—*get back up again!*

Finally, the word *destroy* comes from the Greek word *apollumi,* essentially meaning something that is ruined, wasted, trashed, devastated, and destroyed.

The thief is relentless, and he moves in a strategically diabolical progression. First, he tries to deceptively steal your vision through your thought life. If that doesn't work, he attempts to get you so distracted that you give up your vision. If that plot fails, he then pulls out his most powerful weapons of mass destruction.

The enemy wants to destroy your influence. I've often seen great leaders toppled by the destruction of their reputations. It's one of the devil's deadliest schemes. After years of toiling and building God's Kingdom, some scandal rocks a person's world, and they stop climbing higher to see God's progressive revelation in their latter years.

Perhaps your world has been rocked by scandal. Don't worry, God is the ultimate "fixer." He is able to turn tragedy into triumph! God promoted Joseph from the prison to the palace; he did a makeover on Moses from murderer to deliverer; he transformed Paul from persecutor to preacher! Romans 8:28 reminds us "that God causes everything to work together for the good of those who love God and are called according to his purpose for them." Process is the pathway to purpose!

Power Quote:

The devil can bother you and burden you but he can't beat you! Never, ever, ever give up!

Process: The Vision's Perspective

God told Habakkuk that at the end of the appointed time, the vision would speak and not lie. He didn't say the prophet would speak; He said the *vision* itself would speak; it would testify.

The Greek word for "testimony" is *matureo.* It means "to bear witness… to affirm that one has seen or heard or experienced something, or that…he knows it because taught by divine revelation or inspiration."[7]

When someone or something is tested, there is a challenge or examination, and then results are revealed. The challenge or examination is issued to prove that authentic learning has occurred or, in the case of an object, to verify that what is purported to be, actually is. After the process of testing, if you don't give up in the midst of the struggle, God's word promises that an appointed time is already on God's schedule! At that time, the vision itself will bear witness. It will speak and not lie!

A Time of Prayer

Dear heavenly Father, I thank You and praise You for trusting me through this season. As my faith is being stretched and expanded, and

I declare by faith that it's all working together for my good and for Your glory. I determine now to continue to press forward trusting you with every step on this journey. Father, I am living in hope of the amazing appointed time that shall come; and I submit to and embrace the process. Mold me, shape me, break me, and build me. "Thou art the Potter, I am the clay."[8] In Jesus' name. Amen.

Summary Questions

As you consider the processes you are enduring, carefully and prayerfully answer these questions:

1. How will your vision "testify" that it came out of God and not out of you? What aspects of your vision testify that it was "only" God that orchestrated your success? How has each season of your process prepared you to produce a vision that will testify of God's glory?

2. How has your faith grown during your refining processes?

3. Describe God's kairos moment.

4. How do your prayers reinforce your humility in submission to God's control of time and seasons?

CHAPTER SEVEN

The Principle of Patience: Possessing Vision Requires Patience

Like a storm victim clinging to a tree in the middle of hurricane-force winds; cling to the hope that your vision will become reality. Never let go! —Teresa Hairston

Though it tarries, wait for it; because it will surely come, it will not tarry (Habakkuk 2:3 NKJV).

Dynamic Definition:

Patience (Long-suffering): "…The determination to live by faith and not by feeling, and to respond with grace rather than to react with grief, regardless of the circumstances."[1]

Nelson Mandela (b. 1918) believed that apartheid was wrong and he invested his life fighting it.

"Apartheid" means "apartness" or "separateness" in Afrikaans, [it] was a system of racial segregation that operated in South Africa from 1948 to the early 1990s. Under apartheid the races, classified by law into White, Black, Indian, and Coloured groups, were separated and non-whites were denied voting rights, formal education, medical care, and other public services.[2]

Initially, Mandela led nonviolent protests, but he soon came to believe that armed struggle would be the only way to end apartheid. In 1955, he formed the African National Congress (ANC).

In 1963, as a result of his activism, he and ten other ANC leaders were given life sentences.

The conditions at the prison on Robbins Island (near Cape Town), were so deplorable that Mandela contracted tuberculosis. He spent the next 27 years in prison; but even inside the walls, Mandela increasingly became a beacon of hope and a symbol of the fight for freedom to people across the world.

Finally, in 1990, Mandela, now 71, walked free but the system of apartheid was still in place. Upon his release, he immediately employed every opportunity to renew his fight against apartheid.

The next three years were tense, brutal, and sometimes bloody. Finally, in 1994, Blacks in South Africa won voting rights, public systems of education, and use of public facilities. Mandela's vision had finally come to pass!

The victory over apartheid is a testimony to Mandela's patience, faith, courage, and determination.

Power Quote:

Patience is a narrow pathway not a superhighway. It is dusty, dark, and dangerous; however, it must be deliberately chosen, especially in difficult times if victory is to be achieved. The pathway of patience requires one to walk with discipline and determination, often shedding tears along the way but always trusting in the assurance that at God's appointed time, His promise will be manifest. —Teresa Hairston

Patience Holds Its Position Despite the Struggle

Patience holds its position and maintains its confession, even when it is under pressure or severely challenged. Habakkuk was commanded to wait—to hold his position and maintain his expectation for God's vision to manifest.

Holding your position of faith will often cause you to endure pain and hardship. It isn't pleasant and doesn't feel good; but if you are going to see your vision through from seed to the harvest, you will need patience.

The Bible has a lot to say about patience. In First Corinthians 13:4, love's first attribute is patience. In Galatians 5:22, the fourth character trait of the Holy Spirit is patience. In Romans 15:5, God is described as "the God of patience" (NKJV).

The biblical account of Job stands out as an example of a man who exercised patience in the face of life's most challenging tests. God's vision was for Job to be an example of spiritual fortitude—to remain blameless, faithful to God, and full of integrity, even during catastrophic suffering. In the narrative, when Satan challenged Job's faithfulness under fire, God allowed Satan to devastate Job's wealth, family and health, marriage, and friendships.

Job's response helps us understand how to handle crisis. Although Job was angry, bewildered, and in utter despair, in the midst of his grief and pain he held his position of faith in God's sovereignty. He never sinned and he never stopped acknowledging the wisdom, power, and righteousness of God. He endured the storms.

How will you handle the inevitable crises of your life? What will your response be when you feel anger, bewilderment, and discouragement? It's not a matter of *if,* but *when.* Will you respond with patience or impatience?

The Bible uses the word *longsuffering* almost interchangeably with the word *patience.* "Longsuffering is that quality of self-restraint in the face of provocation which does not hastily retaliate or promptly punish...."[3]

Job was angry but he didn't sin; he was bewildered but he didn't curse God; he was in utter despair but he didn't take his own life!

Instead, Job became the "poster child" of patience—he affirmed that God was still in control and he maintained his belief in the integrity of God's Word.

Can God trust you with trouble? In the midst of your struggle, will you curse and complain, or will you wait?

- Patience is a sign of spiritual maturity.

- Patience waits with expectation in the midst of devastation!

- Patience endures physical, emotional, psychological, and spiritual trauma, and holds onto faith in God.

- Patience speaks faith over facts.

- Patience declares victory, even in the valley of despair.

Patience is bitter, but its fruit is sweet. —Aristotle[4]

Patience Doesn't Ask "How Long?"

Have you ever called a business and reached an automated answering system that took you through a series of prompts before getting you to the right department? Then, instead of getting a live operator, you heard the computerized attendant say, "Your call will be answered in the order it was received." Perhaps you hung up in frustration, or had a bad attitude toward the operator who finally answered.

I want to help you embrace a new paradigm regarding patience and vision.

It is God who is actually being patient! He is literally waiting for you to catch up to what He has already prepared for you! In His infinite wisdom and unfailing love, He knows that if He were to manifest the fullness of your vision before your character is ready to handle it, you would destroy your own future! So He patiently, lovingly waits for you to work through the processes and come to a point of fully surrendering to Him.

The most powerful truth you can embrace as a visionary is that God's timing is perfect! His plan is complete and because of His love for you He is literally waiting for you!

> *The Lord isn't really being slow about his promise, as some people think. No, he is being patient for your sake. He does not want anyone to be destroyed, but wants everyone to repent* (2 Peter 3:9).

Power Quote:

A waiting person is a patient person. The word *patience* means the willingness to stay where we are and live the situation out to the full in the belief that something hidden there will manifest itself to us. —Henri J.M. Nouwen[5]

Patience Protects and Prepares You

One of the greatest benefits of patience is protection. There are things that patience allows you to see—in yourself and in others—that will protect you from future devastation. As you move forward in patient expectation of the appointed time for your vision to fully manifest, you will witness the character and motives of yourself, and learn even more about who you truly are.

In Psalm 31:7-8, David writes:

"I will be glad and rejoice in your unfailing love, for you have seen my troubles, and you care about the anguish of my soul. You have not handed me over to my enemies but have set me in a safe place."

You might think you really know yourself, but every experience opens up more of who you are.

- How do you handle times of sickness?

- How do you handle a doctor's report that confirms disease?

- What do you do when a friend betrays you?

- What do you do when someone disrespects you?

While waiting on God's vision to manifest, strive to grow deeper in God and closer to Him by responding to every challenge and situation in accordance with His word. Protect your future by developing your character now.

Dear brothers and sisters, when troubles come your way, consider it an opportunity for great joy. For you know that when your faith is tested, your endurance has a chance to grow. So let it grow, for when your endurance is fully developed, you will be perfect and complete, needing nothing (James 1:2-4).

What are *your* character flaws? Everyone has them, but most of us see the flaws in others and not ourselves.

Success also exposes character flaws! Many people have climbed the ladder of success only to get to the top and fall!

You may have a great personality, be extremely talented, and possess superior intelligence; but your personality can only open the door. It is your character that will keep you in the room.

Paul wrote: "Examine yourselves to see if your faith is genuine. Test yourselves" (2 Cor. 13:5).

Are you arrogant? Prideful? Selfish? Possessive? Controlling? Do you have secret sin in your life? The sooner you repent, the sooner God will manifest the fullness of vision in your life!

Waiting Impatiently Causes Delays

Here are some signs of "waiting impatiently": You feel that others who are less talented or deserving are doing better than you and moving past you. Your friends are dating and mating while you're still spending nights alone. Colleagues who aren't doing the level of ministry or business with the integrity that you are seem to be getting all the attention and opportunities, while you're stuck on a treadmill going nowhere!

But let me encourage you to wait patiently; here are some affirmations to speak over your life and vision each day:

1. God is faithful and He is just.

God will make this happen, for he who calls you is faithful (1 Thessalonians 5:24).

2. God has not forgotten you.

For God is not unjust. He will not forget how hard you have worked for him and how you have shown your love to him by caring for other believers, as you still do (Hebrews 6:10).

3. What God promises, He will perform.

Understand, therefore, that the Lord your God is indeed God. He is the faithful God who keeps his covenant for a thousand generations and lavishes his unfailing love on those who love him and obey his commands (Deuteronomy 7:9).

4. God is right on schedule. His timing is perfect.

This is the plan: At the right time he will bring everything together under the authority of Christ—everything in heaven and on earth (Ephesians 1:10).

5. It's not too late and you're not "past your prime." Keep trusting. Keep obeying. Keep waiting.

For everything there is a season, a time for every activity under heaven. A time to be born and a time to die. A time to plant and a time to harvest. A time to kill and a time to heal. A time to tear down and a time to build up. A time to cry and a time to laugh. A time to grieve and a time to dance. A time to scatter stones and a time to gather stones. A time to embrace and a time to turn away. A time to search and a time to quit searching. A time to keep and a time to throw away. A time to tear and a time to mend. A time to be quiet and a time to speak. A time to love and a time to hate. A time for war and a time for peace (Ecclesiastes 3:1-8).

A Time of Prayer

Father, You are a God of infinite patience. You have tolerated the imperfections and forgiven the sins of your people throughout the ages, and You've done the same for me.

I know I haven't always been patient with others, with You, or with myself. I often want things to happen immediately. I even try to force things to happen in my own timing. But today, Father, I surrender to Your timing and Your plan.

Right now, I quiet my spirit and I declare that I am anxious for nothing and I trust You for everything. I will wait patiently for You; I will wait with confidence. I will wait joyfully while learning of You and submitting to You. In Jesus' name I pray. Amen.

Summary Questions

1. Do you consider yourself impatient or patient? In what areas of your life do you exhibit the most patience? In what areas of your life do you exhibit the least?

2. What experiences (personal, professional, physical, emotional, etc.) have taught you to be patient? Write three of these lessons in a journal. Keep the journal as a reflection point for the future.

3. What scriptures speak directly to your current stage of growth regarding patience? Take time to copy and paste these scriptures into your phone notepad; review the scriptures daily for the next 30 days until you have them memorized. These scriptures will become your provision and protection.

Phase Four: WALKING

Passion

"Behold the proud..."

Productivity

"His soul is not upright in him..."

Perseverance

"but the just shall live by his faith" (Habakkuk 2:4 NKJV).

CHAPTER EIGHT

The Principle of Passion: You Are Driven by Your Heart's Desire

God will give you the desires of your heart—this means He will place the "right" passions within your heart. —Teresa Hairston

Behold the proud
(Habakkuk 2:4 NKJV).

Dynamic Definition:

Passion: A boundless, overwhelming emotion; such as love, joy, hatred, or anger.

Mother Teresa was a woman small in stature, but with a gigantic love for the poor.

Born Agnes Gonxha Bojaxhiu in Albania in 1910, Mother Teresa was raised in a devout Catholic family. When she was eight, her father died unexpectedly, and she became very close to her mother. Although the family had meager means, her mother, who often took in and fed strangers, counseled her, saying, "My child, never eat a single mouthful unless you are sharing it with others."[1]

At the age of 18, Agnes accepted her call to religious service and became a nun. She moved to Ireland and joined the Loreto Sisters of Dublin where she took on the name *Teresa* (after Saint Thérèse of Lisieux) and received the title *Mother* after completing her Final Profession of Vows to a life of poverty. Her first assignment to teach at a high school in Calcutta, India, introduced her to abject poverty. In 1946, her life changed forever.

She [Mother Teresa] was riding a train from Calcutta to the Himalayan foothills for a retreat when Christ spoke to her and told her to abandon teaching to work in the slums of Calcutta aiding the city's poorest and sickest people. She heard Christ say to her on the train that day, "You are I know the most incapable person— weak and sinful but just because you are that—I want to use You for My glory. Wilt thou refuse?"[2]

It took two years for Mother Teresa to convince her local archbishop to grant her permission to pursue this new mission. When she was released, her passion for her call was amazing.

In October 1950, she started her new congregation, the Missionaries of Charity, with only 12 members. Over the next two decades, she established a leper colony, an orphanage, a nursing home, a family clinic, and a string of mobile health clinics.

In February 1965, Pope John Paul VI bestowed the Decree of Praise upon the Missionaries of Charity, which prompted Mother Teresa to begin expanding internationally. In 1979, she was awarded the Nobel Peace Prize in recognition of her work "in bringing help to suffering humanity."[3] By the time of her death in 1997, the Missionaries of Charity numbered over 4,000, with thousands more lay volunteers and 610 foundations in 123 countries on all seven continents.

Mother Teresa was incredibly successful, however despite the enormous scale of her charitable activities and the millions of lives she touched, to her dying day she held only the most humble conception of her own achievements. Her admonition to others: "Learn to do ordinary things with extraordinary love," inspired millions.

"Not all of us can do great things. But we can do small things with great love." —Mother Teresa[4]

Passion's Daring Look at the Proud

For the first time in our Vision Model, God instructs us to look around instead of up. He says, "Look at the proud!" This indicates that God has prepared us spiritually to handle what we will see in the natural realm and still move forward in obedience to the Holy Spirit.

This look at the proud shows us everything we should *not* aspire to be, have or do. *Pride, a heightened and inflated sense of self-worth, arrogance, haughtiness or conceit, is the most deadly of sins.* It corrupts, infects, and destroys everything it touches. Pride separates us from God.

The Bible shows us a portrait of pride in Ezekiel 28:12-18. In this passage, God speaks prophetically to the coming destruction of a king who allowed pride to infest his heart. The passage parallels the king with Lucifer, the fallen angel.

> *Son of man, sing this funeral song for the king of Tyre. Give him this message from the Sovereign Lord: "You were the model of perfection, full of wisdom and exquisite in beauty. You were in Eden, the garden of God. Your clothing was adorned with every precious stone—red carnelian, pale-green peridot, white moonstone, blue-green beryl, onyx, green jasper, blue lapis lazuli, turquoise, and emerald—all beautifully crafted for you and set in the finest gold. They were given to you on the day you were created. I ordained and anointed you as the mighty angelic guardian. You had access to the holy mountain of God and walked among the stones of fire. You were blameless in all you did from the day you were created until the day evil was found in you. Your rich commerce led you to violence, and you sinned. So I banished you in disgrace from the mountain of God. I expelled you, O mighty guardian, from your place among the stones of fire. Your heart was filled with pride because of all your beauty. Your wisdom was corrupted by your love of splendor. So I threw you to the ground and exposed you to the curious gaze of kings. You defiled your sanctuaries with your many sins and your dishonest trade. So I brought fire out from within you, and it consumed you. I reduced you to ashes on the ground in the sight of all who were watching."*

Pride corrupts God's blessings. He was:

- The model of perfection

- Full of wisdom and exquisite in beauty

- Adorned magnificently

- Ordained and anointed by God

- Given access to God's inner court

- Initially blameless

Pride ruins everything: "Your rich commerce led you to violence, and you sinned" (v. 16). As a result of a "heart filled with pride" God did the following:

- Banished him from the mountain of God

- Expelled him

- Threw him to the ground

- Exposed him

- Humiliated him ("I reduced you to ashes on the ground in the sight of all who were watching")

Most Christians love to focus on the gentle, loving, patient character of God; but we need to look at the whole picture. God is kind, but he will not tolerate the sin of pride.

> *How you are fallen from heaven, O shining star, son of the morning! You have been thrown down to the earth, you who destroyed the nations of the world. For you said to yourself, "I will ascend to heaven and set my throne above God's stars. I will preside on the mountain of the gods far away in the north I will climb to the highest heavens and be like the Most High." Instead, you will be brought down to the place of the dead, down to its lowest depths* (Isaiah 14:12-15).

The "I wills" of Lucifer reveal the true passions of his heart. Lucifer's pride made him so ambitious that he dared to be like God! Pride is deadly!

Passion Out of Control Turns to Perversion

As you walk the road of vision, it is essential to consistently examine your motives along the way. There are times, especially in the beginning of the journey when your prayers, thoughts, and motives are grounded in humility. However, along the way, especially in times of prosperity, it can be extremely difficult to keep your spirit, flesh, and emotions humble.

There are various types of pride:

Spiritual pride. People infected with spiritual pride believe that they deserve to be more prosperous and more blessed than others because they live holier lives.

The Pharisees of biblical times were a self-righteous sect of religious leaders. In Luke 18:9-14, Jesus shared a parable about a Pharisee and a tax collector who went to pray in the Temple. The Pharisee was diligent in keeping all the laws of the Torah. By contrast, the tax collectors of those times were known as dishonest people of low moral standards. The Pharisee prayed long and loud, arrogantly emphasizing his righteousness compared with those around him as a justification for his elevated spiritual status. But the tax collector prayed a simple prayer of humility: "O God, be merciful to me, for I am a sinner" (verse 13).

Jesus concluded the lesson by saying:

I tell you, this sinner, not the Pharisee, returned home justified before God. For those who exalt themselves will be humbled, and those who humble themselves will be exalted (Luke 18:14).

Physical pride. This person is driven by a desire for money and the material possessions it can buy, as well as an overemphasis on natural and physical beauty.

There has always been a lot of conversation and concern regarding Christians with money. Let me affirm that there is nothing wrong with having money; in fact, it's wonderful to be financially secure and even prosperous, as long as you remember to honor God's Word in how you manage and invest your money.

When it comes to any symbols of success that we might own—expensive luxury cars, large homes, technological gadgets, and beautiful clothes—it is easy for these items to take possession of us. Many people live to gain "things" and almost "kill themselves" trying to keep them. This is often true even for those who don't have the means to pay for or maintain these items.

Physical beauty can become addictive. Some people spend thousands upon thousands of dollars to enhance their outer appearance or exercise "religiously."

While it is not sinful to live in luxury or be beautiful, the Bible speaks directly to having a passion or love for these things:

> *Do not love this world nor the things it offers you, for when you love the world, you do not have the love of the Father in you. For the world offers only a craving for physical pleasure, a craving for everything we see, and pride in our achievements and possessions. These are not from the Father, but are from this world. And this world is fading away, along with everything that people crave. But anyone who does what pleases God will live forever* (1 John 2:15-17).

Emotional pride. When you become used to being acknowledged, honored, served, and celebrated, you will be tempted to adapt a spirit of emotional arrogance. The temptation is subtle; it sneaks up on you when you're least vigilant. One day, you find yourself *expecting* to be recognized and *looking* for people to applaud you.

Proverbs 16:18 is very clear: "Pride goes before destruction, and a haughty spirit before a fall" (NKJV). This verse is saying almost the same thing twice, as pride and a haughty spirit are virtually identical, as are destruction and stumbling.

Proverbs 29:23 states: "Pride ends in humiliation, while humility brings honor."

In the New Testament, Jesus listed the evil things that defile a man. These things are the symptoms of a heart that has been infected with the sin of pride.

> *For from within, out of a person's heart, come evil thoughts, sexual immorality, theft, murder, adultery, greed, wickedness, deceit, lustful desires, envy, slander, pride, and foolishness. All these vile things come from within; they are what defile you* (Mark 7:21-23).

Notice that in this same list with pride are murder, sexual immorality, and foolishness. *Pride is spiritually, physically, and emotionally destructive!*

Passion Requires Suffering

Mother Teresa is unquestionably inspiring. She is a woman who gave her life in passionate service to others. However, one of the most shocking revelations about her came after she died.

In 2003, a publication of her private correspondence revealed that she had lived most of her last fifty years suffering a crisis of faith.

> In one despairing letter to a confidante she wrote, "Where is my Faith—even deep down right in there is nothing, but emptiness & darkness—My God—how painful is this unknown pain—I have no Faith—I dare not utter the words & thoughts that crowd in my heart—& make me suffer untold agony."[5]

Mother Teresa' crisis of faith reveals her humility; but it also portrays a woman who continued to walk forward in her vision despite the suffering. Her passion for God's vision overrode her personal feelings.

In Philippians 2, we see a powerful look at passion through the agony of Jesus. In the 2004 movie, *The Passion of the Christ,* millions of people were riveted with the detailed account of the crucifixion of Jesus.

Although the Bible doesn't tell us all that Jesus thought about in His last days and hours on Earth, it does tell us what Jesus said. Matthew 27:46 provides this record:

> *At about three o'clock, Jesus called out with a loud voice, "Eli, Eli, lema sabachthani?" which means "My God, my God, why have you abandoned me?"*

Jesus was necessarily abandoned yet simultaneously empowered by His Father so that He could bear the sins of the world. The emptiness and darkness that He must have felt as he hung there in agony was incomprehensible; but equally incomprehensible was the joy He must have felt by fulfilling His passion and saving the world.

The passion you have for the vision God has invested in you will require suffering; there's no way around it. As you walk forward, face your future with the confidence that God's provision will elevate you as you humbly submit to His will.

A Time of Prayer

Father, I thank and praise You for the opportunity and privilege of being called, anointed, and appointed as Your servant. I humbly embrace this vision for my life; and I ask You to search me, God, and know my heart; examine my thoughts, and show me, me! I want to serve You with all my heart and mind and strength. Cleanse me now, oh God…in Jesus' name. Amen!

Summary Questions

1. What is your passion? What is your cause? What are your true motives?

2. Do you have areas of pride that you need to repent of? Are there secret sins in your life that you need to forsake?

3. Compare your spiritual, physical, and emotional philosophies to God's Word. Are you truly able to say that you're living in humility, integrity and love? If not, commit these things to prayer and commit your thoughts, words, and actions to change.

4. Write a list of the specific areas of your life where you are struggling with pride. Make a prayer and action plan to replace those areas of pride with godly humility.

CHAPTER NINE

The Principle of Productivity:
Right Motives Produce Right Results

Godly productivity results when all your external resources are submitted to the internal leading of the Holy Spirit. —*Teresa Hairston*

His soul is not upright in him
(Habakkuk 2:4 NKJV).

Dynamic Definition:

Productivity: "the quality, state, or fact of being able to generate, create, enhance, or bring forth goods and services...."[1]

Apostle Paul was one of the most phenomenal men who ever lived. He began his life as Saul of Tarsus. In his pre-conversion days, Saul's family was well off and very religious. His father was a member of the respected Pharisee sect (the respected experts in Old Testament law), and when Saul was a young man, his parents sent him off to a prestigious school in Jerusalem to study so that he could become a Pharisee. (See Acts 23:6; Philippians 3:5; Acts 22:3.)

Saul completed his schooling, became a Pharisee, and was zealous to defend his traditional, Old Testament beliefs. He enlisted in a campaign to stamp out Christianity. He actively sought out and arrested Christians for practicing their beliefs through a "by any means necessary" approach.

Paul became part of brutal, no-holds-barred, hate-filled torture missions in which Christians were often beaten and sometimes killed.

According to the traditions of the day, Saul had a great foundation; but he was on the wrong road according to God's transformative vision for his life. He was an example of a man whose "soul is not upright."

However, when Saul experienced God's vision and heard God's words on the Damascus Road, his disposition changed. Although he was totally baffled (which is *always* the case with God's vision), he submitted himself to God. His response exemplifies how we should respond to vision. "So he [Saul], trembling and astonished, said, 'Lord, what do You want me to do?'" (Acts 9:6 NKJV)

- Saul didn't spend time talking to others to share the news of the encounter.

- Saul didn't try to analyze his human senses to "figure out" whether the encounter was authentic.

- Saul didn't push back with human reasoning as to the best strategy for implementing God's instruction.

- Saul humbled himself and obeyed. Then, for a period of time, he availed his spirit to the Holy Spirit to reteach and retrain him for the season ahead. He even accepted God's new name—Paul.

God had a huge assignment for Paul's life. He used everything Paul had learned and experienced, as well as every skill, talent, and gift to accomplish the assignment. And Paul submitted.

In the end, God's vision for Paul to become the greatest missionary who ever lived was fufilled. Paul became an instrument of mercy to all men, especially to the Gentiles (see Acts 9:15; 22:15; 26:17).

Paul's productivity in the service of God changed the world. He conducted three missionary journeys during which he departed radically from the tradition of sharing the Gospel only with the Jews to the model of preaching the Gospel of Jesus Christ to transform the lives of the Gentiles. He planted churches throughout Asia Minor, Greece, and Rome. He also wrote essential doctrinal letters that today comprise approximately half (13 of 27 books) of the New Testament.

Power Quote:

The best way to succeed is to have a specific Intent, a clear Vision, a plan of Action, and the ability to maintain Clarity. Those are the Four Pillars of Success. It never fails! —Steve Maraboli[2]

Productivity Prevails over Adversity

Paul's productivity was undaunted by adversity. The Bible reports that Paul endured tremendous hardship *after* he submitted to God's vision for his life.

- Immediately after he was converted, he was targeted for assassination. Christians were so fearful of him and skeptical about his conversion that they plotted to kill him (see Acts 9:22-25; 2 Cor. 11:32).

- He was rejected. He went to Jerusalem to try to meet with the disciples, but initially, they didn't believe his conversion and wouldn't meet with him (see Acts 9:26).

- He was persecuted for being obedient. After preaching in Jerusalem, another faction tried to kill him. He had to flee for his life (see Acts 9:29-30).

- God allowed him to suffer. Paul had a physical ailment (some say malaria). He referred to it as a thorn in his flesh and asked God three times to remove it. His request was denied (see 2 Cor. 12:7-9).

- He experienced overwhelming hardships. Paul was beaten, shipwrecked, imprisoned, bitten by a snake (see Acts 28:3), and ostracized by other Christian leaders.

In Second Corinthians 11:24-27 Paul testified:

Five different times the Jewish leaders gave me thirty-nine lashes. Three times I was beaten with rods. Once I was stoned. Three times I was shipwrecked. Once I spent a whole night and a day adrift at sea. I have traveled on many long journeys. I have faced danger from rivers and from robbers. I have faced danger from my own people, the Jews, as well as from the Gentiles. I have faced danger in the cities, in the deserts, and on the seas. And I have faced danger from men who claim to be believers but are not. I have worked hard and long, enduring many sleepless nights. I have been hungry and thirsty and have often gone without food. I have shivered in the cold, without enough clothing to keep me warm.

Every person who has faith in his or her vision will encounter adversity. It is inevitable, and it never stops. The bigger your vision, the greater the adversity you'll face. The key to handling adversity is to allow it to strengthen you, not stop you.

Know, by faith, that God is greater than any adversity you will ever face.

You belong to God, my dear children. You have already won a victory over those people, because the Spirit who lives in you is greater than the spirit who lives in the world (1 John 4:4).

Power Quote:

Time is the great leveler. It is one resource that is allocated in absolute egalitarian terms. Every living person has the same number of hours to use in every day. Busy people are not given a special bonus added on to the hours of the day. The clock plays no favorites. —Dr. R.C. Sproul[3]

Productivity Prevails over Procrastination

As you pursue your vision, one of the great enemies of productivity will be procrastination. Putting off for tomorrow what you can do today can become a way of life. Eventually your mind can get so clouded that you develop a "block," and end up putting your vision aside with the famous Schwarzenegger promise: "I'll be back!"

If you are a procrastinator, you fall into the category of one whose "soul is not upright." The enemy literally has you twisted. You have fallen into his trap of laziness, fear, or sloppiness. One of the shrewd tactics of the enemy is to get you to procrastinate in "just" a few areas, while remaining productive in others. Before you know it, the procrastination becomes like a cancer spreading to more and more areas of your life and vision; contaminating, crippling or destroying your future. If you recognize procrastination in any arena of your life, make the necessary corrections immediately!

The opposite of procrastination is diligence and the Bible teaches us that this quality is a key to success:

Spiritual diligence is exemplified by Jesus' diligence in prayer to His Father: "Before daybreak the next morning, Jesus got up and went out to an isolated place to pray" (Mark 1:35).

Vocational diligence is shown by Solomon's diligent obedience to God's instructions in building the Temple:

Now seek the Lord your God with all your heart and soul. Build the sanctuary of the Lord God so that you can bring the Ark of the Lord's Covenant and the holy vessels of God into the Temple built to honor the Lord's name (1 Chronicles 22:19).

When you study Solomon's attention to detail in building the Temple, you will get a true picture of the type of detail required to fulfill God's vision with excellence. Diligence leads to excellence and God rewards diligence. "Do you see any truly competent workers? They will serve kings rather than working for ordinary people" (Prov. 22:29).

God instructs us to be *diligent in our faith:*

It is impossible to please God without faith. Anyone who wants to come to him must believe that God exists and that he rewards those who sincerely seek him (Hebrews 11:6).

Power Quote:

Your vision will become clear only when you look into your heart. Who looks outside, dreams; who looks inside awakens. —Carl Jung[4]

Productivity Listens for God's "Now" Rather Than His "Then"

Vision always gives a picture of the future. Habakkuk submitted to God's vision, which was for the future. If you do not submit to God's vision, you will operate in the past or present and miss your future harvest.

When I was growing up, I was mesmerized by television. Although our family only had a black and white TV with a small screen of only about 15 inches, it connected me to a world of images, information, and inspiration. I remember Walter Cronkite giving the news, Johnny Carson telling jokes and wearing crazy costumes on *The Tonight Show,* Ed Sullivan introducing a variety of entertainers, and many other shows that I enjoyed watching. I was thoroughly entertained.

However, television at best shows the past and the present; it never shows the future. TV producers spend millions of dollars every year to capture the attention of the public, but entertainment runs in cycles and seasons that come to a dead end. Walter Cronkite, Johnny Carson, and Ed Sullivan have all made their final transitions; none of their shows have remained popular. However, God's vision produces fruit that yields endless harvest.

Jesus says in John 15:1-2:

> *I am the true grapevine, and my Father is the gardener. He cuts off every branch of mine that doesn't produce fruit, and he prunes the branches that do bear fruit so they will produce even more.*

The Grapevine (Jesus) is the source of connection between the Gardener (God) and the branches (you and me) that produce fruit. God doesn't *hope* we'll produce, He fully *expects and equips* us to produce; in fact, if we do *not* produce, we will be cut off!

Being productive for God means fulfilling vision; you can only fulfill vision when there is nothing hindering the flow of God's voice in your life. Oftentimes, your past will hold your future hostage if you allow it; you will stop at "yesterday" and never turn the page to get to "tomorrow." Here are some guidelines to help you break through to godly productivity:

1. *Obey God, no matter how crazy you might look.* Noah built an ark in the middle of the desert, even though it had never rained before. Obey God and don't worry about what your friends

and family say. "So Noah did everything exactly as God had commanded him" (Gen. 6:22). God told Ezekiel to lie on his left side for 390 days (Ezek. 4:4), and then on his right side for another 40 days (Ezek. 4:6) as a symbolic gesture to highlight Israel and Judah's sins. God also told him to bake cakes using human waste as the "charcoal" of choice (Ezek. 4:12) and that he was to bake these cakes in the sight of the people.

God told Isaiah to walk around naked and barefoot for three years (see Isa. 20:1).

God told Hosea to marry a prostitute (see Hos 1:2).

God's instructions might initially seem crazy, but they will have a powerful impact on future nations and generations.

2. *Guard your heart, even if it makes you unpopular.* Your level of productivity will increase when you carefully guard what you look at, what you listen to, and the company you keep. In Psalm 101:3-7, David wrote:

I hate all who deal crookedly; I will have nothing to do with them. I will reject perverse ideas and stay away from every evil. I will not tolerate people who slander their neighbors. I will not endure conceit and pride. I will search for faithful people to be my companions. Only those who are above reproach will be allowed to serve me. I will not allow deceivers to serve in my house, and liars will not stay in my presence.

As you concern yourself with the highest levels of productivity, you must remember that you never have to compromise God's way to accomplish God's will.

3. *Be careful who you connect with.*

Beware of false prophets who come disguised as harmless sheep but are really vicious wolves. You can identify them by their fruit, that is, by the way they act. Can you pick grapes from thornbushes, or figs from thistles? A good tree produces good fruit, and a bad tree produces bad fruit. A good tree can't produce bad fruit, and a bad tree can't produce good fruit. So every tree that does not produce good fruit is chopped down and thrown into the fire. Yes, just as you can identify a tree by its fruit, so you can identify people by their actions (Matthew 7:15-20).

4. *If you've fallen, get back up and move forward.* Productivity isn't about perfection, it's about perseverance. You will make mistakes. Some mistakes can make you want to lay down and never get back up again; but you can and you must. Every lesson you've learned in the grip of failure will provide strength for your future. Your misery will produce ministry. Allow God to reshape, renew, and reposition you.

So take a new grip with your tired hands and strengthen your weak knees. Mark out a straight path for your feet so that those who are weak and lame will not fall but become strong (Hebrews 12:12-13).

A Time of Prayer

Father, I thank You for Your vision for my life and I thank You for Your supply of everything I need to accomplish that vision. I confess that many of my past thoughts, words, and actions have not been pleasing in your sight; but today I humbly surrender all to You—my life, heart, mind, soul, and strength. I pray for restoration in every area.

I thank You for being a loving, faithful God. I thank You that You have never stopped loving me, and that You have always been there—ready, willing, and able to renew and revive me. Father, I submit to Your leadership today.

Thank You for this new season, filled with new opportunities, new relationships, and new victories. In the name of Jesus, I now take authority over and bind the enemy that seeks to fill my mind with thoughts of distraction, defeat, and discouragement. His assignment to confuse me and to cause me to fail is cancelled! He has no place or power in my life. I am free! I am renewed by the blood of Jesus. I am an overcomer through the blood of the Lamb! In Jesus' name. Amen!

Summary Questions

1. In what area of your life and vision have you faced the most adversity? What has God shown you about that area? If you don't know, take time to fast, pray, and hear God on this matter—He will speak, just listen.

2. Are there areas in your life and vision where you have procrastinated? What are the reasons? Find scriptural answers that speak to the solutions to your problems.

3. What is God telling you to do in your next season? What about His "progressive revelation" is different from your last season?

4. Are there areas of your life and vision that have suffered in productivity due to: 1) disobedience, 2) double-mindedness, 3) deceptive friends/associates, 4) personal/professional devastation? What will you do to "correct" these things?

CHAPTER TEN

The Principle of Perseverance:
Never Let Go of Your Vision!

*If you faithfully persevere in the plan of God; you will surely
reap the promise of God. —Teresa Hairston*

*Behold the proud, His soul is not upright in him;
but the just shall live by his faith* (Habakkuk 2:4 NKJV).

Dynamic Definition:

Perseverance: "Steady persistence in adhering to a course of action, a
belief, or a purpose; steadfastness."[1] "Continuance in a given course of
action in the face of difficulty or opposition."

Caleb is one of the most inspiring and intriguing people of the Bible.
Over two million Israelites left Egypt, but amazingly, he and Joshua were
the only two who actually entered the Promised Land. Joshua was Moses'
understudy, chosen to lead the people into the new land; but who was
Caleb?

The Bible says Caleb "had a different spirit and followed God fully" (see
Num. 14:24). The name *Caleb* means "wholehearted" or "faithful," and he
certainly lived up to his name. In Numbers 13:30, after he and 11 others
returned from their assignment to spy out the Promised Land, Caleb was

the first to bring a positive report: "'Let's go at once to take the land,' he said. 'We can certainly conquer it!'"

Unfortunately, ten other spies had negative reports and spoke fear into the hearts of the people. As a result, the people doubted God and wavered in their faith and God allowed them to wander in the wilderness 40 years. However, Caleb never gave up on the promise—he never stopped believing!

Along the journey, Moses made a promise of land to Caleb. This land was important, because it would become an inheritance to his family.

Finally, after entering the Promised Land, the Israelites prepared to divide the territories and give portions to the various tribes. Caleb was ready! He refused to be forgotten or left out; he spoke up to lay claim to his promise.

> *Now, as you can see, the Lord has kept me alive and well as he promised for all these forty-five years since Moses made this promise—even while Israel wandered in the wilderness. Today I am eighty-five years old. I am as strong now as I was when Moses sent me on that journey, and I can still travel and fight as well as I could then. So give me the hill country that the Lord promised me* (Joshua 14:10-12).

The King James Version of verse 12 reads: "Now therefore give me this mountain…."

Caleb claimed his promise! "So Joshua blessed Caleb son of Jephunneh and gave Hebron to him as his portion of land" (Josh. 14:13).

The lessons of Caleb's life reinforce the principle of perseverance:

1. God rewards faithful perseverance with fulfilled promises.

> *God is not a man, so he does not lie. He is not human, so he does not change his mind. Has he ever spoken and failed to act? Has he ever promised and not carried it through?* (Numbers 23:19).

2. Persevere and never give up! God's promises don't have an expiration date.

He who is the Glory of Israel does not lie or change his mind; for he is not a human being, that he should change his mind (1 Samuel 15:29 NIV).

3. You can trust the promise of God. Although you persevere for a lifetime, not one of God's promises will ever fail.

I will maintain my love to him forever, and my covenant with him will never fail (Psalm 89:28 NIV).

Perseverance Walks by Faith, Not Fact

Never fact-check God!

When Moses was told by God to go and possess the Promised Land, *why* did he send a posse to check out the land?

Human nature says, "Let me research this business idea. Let me talk to my advisors first. Let me check out the average revenues for this area of enterprise."

Faith says, "If God said it, that settles it, I'm going for it!"

Faith is the confidence that what we hope for will actually happen; it gives us assurance about things we cannot see (Hebrews 11:1).

In Genesis, God told Sarah she would conceive a child at the age of 90. Sarah had lived her life in acceptance of the fact that she was barren. Although she and Abraham wanted to have children, they had not been able to. They were thrilled when God gave them the news, but they were challenged to persevere by faith, believing what God said until God was prepared for the promise to manifest. Sarah messed up and pushed her husband toward another woman. She was eager to "help" God.

God's promises don't depend on facts, research, or your assistance! God's promises operate as a result of His sovereignty. In your efforts to help God, you will often end up getting in your own way and frustrating the work of grace in your life.

Paul writes:

Is the law, therefore, opposed to the promises of God? Absolutely not! For if a law had been given that could impart life, then righteousness would certainly have come by the law (Galatians 3:21 NIV).

God doesn't need your help! Research is good and wise counsel is wonderful, but God's Word never aligns with *what is;* it always defines *what will be!*

Perseverance Chooses Faith over Fear

Fear is one of the biggest obstacles to vision. As humans, we are conditioned to fear the unknown. It's normal for us to want to be in control of the circumstances surrounding us. The average person wants to be in charge of his or her own destiny.

The Bible says that Caleb wholeheartedly believed God's promise. He was one man in a nation of over two million people; they all believed and acted one way, but he believed something different!

He chose to keep believing, despite what everyone else was saying and doing. When Aaron made the golden calf and the people worshipped the calf, Caleb chose to worship God. When the people murmured and complained and tried to get Caleb to agree, he chose to speak faith in God.

Caleb's choices determined his destiny. Your choices will determine *your* destiny.

Going against the grain, not fitting in, being a one-man or one-woman band is difficult. You will often feel alone, isolated, and ostracized. Those feelings open the door to doubt and fear; but if you are to succeed in fulfilling God's vision for your life totally and completely, you will have to divorce doubt and crucify fear. It's your choice!

In Hebrews 11:23, Moses' parents overcame fear and followed the vision of God:

By faith Moses' parents hid him for three months after he was born, because they saw he was no ordinary child, and they were not afraid of the king's edict (NIV).

How far outside of your 'comfort zone' will you walk by faith? When God said, "The just shall live by his faith," he defined the just as those who choose to submit their lives to His Word, His Way, and His will. "My righteous ones will live by faith. But I will take no pleasure in anyone who turns away" (Heb. 10:38).

To live a life that pleases God, you must choose to persevere despite the challenges and changes around you. You must remain steadfast and unmoveable in your faith.

To walk by faith means to choose the path of resistance much of the time. It means choosing the road of discomfort and the way of loneliness. But as you walk forward with confidence in God, you will find that He will reward you with assurance in every step of your journey.

Perseverance Runs the Entire Race

I'm sure there were times when Caleb (who was a real man, made of flesh and blood) had a fleeting thought to give up on God's promise. Forty-five years is a long time! But in his wholehearted faithfulness, he never allowed any thought contrary to God's Word to take root in his heart.

The Apostle Paul wrote in Second Corinthians 10:4: "We use God's mighty weapons, not worldly weapons, to knock down the strongholds of human reasoning and to destroy false arguments."

How can you fight and win against all the tactics the enemy uses to try to make you quit? Knowing that you have a great vision isn't enough. Having talent or a great personality isn't enough. Having experience or intelligence isn't enough. Having money or powerful connections isn't enough!

You will need the power of God to sustain you. God's power resides in two agents: God's Word and the person of the Holy Spirit.

1. God's Word will sustain you, because it contains God's power.

Oh, the joys of those who do not follow the advice of the wicked, or stand around with sinners, or join in with mockers. But they delight in the law of the Lord, meditating on it day and night. They are like trees planted along the riverbank, bearing fruit each season. Their leaves never wither, and they prosper in all they do (Psalm 1:1-3).

2. The Holy Spirit is the agent of God's power in the earth.

When the Spirit of truth comes, he will guide you into all truth. He will not speak on his own but will tell you what he has heard. He will tell you about the future. He will bring me glory by telling you whatever he receives from me (John 16:13-14).

Here's how God's power is made available in your spiritual weaponry:

1. *Truth.* When you speak and live by the truth of God's Word, you release life-giving power from your mouth into your life and vision.

For the word of God is alive and powerful. It is sharper than the sharpest two-edged sword, cutting between soul and spirit, between joint and marrow. It exposes our innermost thoughts and desires (Hebrews 4:12).

You will know the truth, and the truth will set you free (John 8:32).

2. *Love.* When you learn to love like God loves, that kind of love is overwhelming and transformative to everything it touches.

Love is patient, love is kind. It does not envy, it does not boast, it is not proud. It does not dishonor others, it is not self-seeking, it is not easily angered, it keeps no record of wrongs. Love does not delight in evil but rejoices with the truth. It always protects, always trusts, always hopes, always perseveres. Love never fails (1 Corinthians 13:4-8 NIV).

3. *Righteousness.* God shows favor to the righteous.

There is joy for those who deal justly with others and always do what is right (Psalm 106:3).

4. *Faith/prayer.* When your prayers align with God's Word, will, and way, and when they are offered in unwavering faith, the Bible says that God will hear and answer. "The earnest prayer of a righteous person has great power and produces wonderful results" (James 5:16).

As you persevere in your journey of vision, remember to trust God as you take each step forward.

Never give up, no matter what happens. Remember, God made you an overcomer!

> *No, despite all these things, overwhelming victory is ours through Christ, who loved us. And I am convinced that nothing can ever separate us from God's love. Neither death nor life, neither angels nor demons, neither our fears for today nor our worries about tomorrow—not even the powers of hell can separate us from God's love. No power in the sky above or in the earth below—indeed, nothing in all creation will ever be able to separate us from the love of God that is revealed in Christ Jesus our Lord* (Romans 8:37-39).

> *So let's not get tired of doing what is good. At just the right time we will reap a harvest of blessing if we don't give up* (Galatians 6:9).

Closing Thoughts

Habakkuk's life and words will help you walk out the vision for your life. I have lived by them for decades! However, as you finish reading this book, I encourage you to put it in a safe place for retrieval along your journey and in each progressive season of your vision.

In God-visions, there are times when it seems like you are starting all over again. These times need not be frustrating; they are evolutionary—signaling that you are growing in God's grace.

When it's time for you to step into the next season, you will need to do the following:

- **Refocus**. Take time to get away from everything and everyone, and spend time with God.

- **Renew**. Allow God to renew you in the places where you've experienced pain, loss, and disappointment.

- **Reevaluate**. God is so amazing that He always graciously allows us to reevaluate the relationships, thoughts, and actions that find us in the place we are.

- **Rearrange**. Once you reevaluate, you will come up with some answers. Some decisions will be difficult, but make them—and don't flinch!

- **Restrain**. Prepare for victory by humbling yourself. Remember, God never wants to humiliate you.

- **Resist**. Don't give the enemy any ground in your life. Bind every demonic assignment, in the name of Jesus.

Finally, make your way prosperous and enjoy good success by being a private success first and foremost, without seeking public notoriety. Walk in integrity and allow God to supply every need according to His riches in glory—where nothing is lacking or broken!

May God richly bless you!
Teresa Hairston

Endnotes

Preface

"Helen Keller Quotes," Goodreads, http://www.goodreads.com/author/quotes/7275.Helen_Keller (accessed August 24, 2013).

1. Merriam-Webster Online, *Merriam-Webster Online Dictionary* 2013, s.v. "glimpse," http://www.merriam-webster.com/dictionary/glimpse?show=0&t=1377808039 (accessed August 24, 2013).

Introduction

1. Biblesoft's New Exhaustive Strong's Numbers and Concordance with Expanded Greek-Hebrew Dictionary. CD-ROM. Biblesoft, Inc. and International Bible Translators, Inc. (© 1994, 2003, 2006) s.v. "'esher" (OT 835).

2. "Biography for Billy Wilder," IMDb, http://www.imdb.com/name/nm0000697/bio (accessed August 29, 2013).

3. "Winston Churchill Quotes, Goodreads, https://www.goodreads.com/author/quotes/14033.Winston_Churchill (accessed August 29, 2013).

4. Biblesoft's New Exhaustive Strong's, s.v. "chabaq" (OT 2263).

Chapter One—The Principle of Positioning:
Humility Positions You to See Vision

1. *Blue Letter Bible,* Dictionary and Word Search for *"tapeinophrosynē"* (Strong's NT 5012), 1996-2013, http://www.blueletterbible. org/lang/lexicon/lexicon.cfm?Strongs=G5012&t=KJV (accessed August 29, 2013).

2. "50 Awesome Quotes on Vision," Innovation Excellence, http:// www.innovationexcellence.com/blog/2010/11/22/50-awe some-quotes-on-vision/ (accessed August 29, 2013).

Chapter Two—The Principle of Preparation:
God's Wisdom Sharpens Your Vision

1. Merriam-Webster Online, s.v. "preparation," http://www.mer riam-webster.com/dictionary/preparation (August 29, 2013).

2. "Eagle Eyes" *The Eagle's Advocate: Ornithology,* http://members .aol.com/egladvocat/ornith.html#eyes (accessed August 29, 2013).

3. Biblesoft's New Exhaustive Strong's, s.v. "tsaphah" (OT 6822).

4. J. I. Packer, *Knowing God* (City: Publisher, Year), 80.

5. Caty, Medrano, "Top 10 Strong Human Fears," ListVerse, http://listverse.com/2011/09/30/top-10-strong-human-fears/ (accessed August 29, 2013).

6. "Michelangelo Buonarroti Quotes," Goodreads, http://www .goodreads.com/author/quotes/182763.Michelangelo _Buonarroti (accessed August 29, 2013).

Chapter Three—The Principle of Perspective:
Mature Faith Produces Divine Perspective

1. Wordsmyth, s.v. "perspective," http://www.wordsmyth.net/ ?rid=30732 (accessed August 29, 2013).

2. Stephen R. Covey, *The 7 Habits of Highly Effective People: Powerful Lessons in Personal Change* (New York: Simon & Schuster, 2004), 18.

3. "Martin Luther King, Jr. Quotes," BrainyQuote, http://www .brainyquote.com/quotes/authors/m/martin_luther_king _jr.html (August 29, 2013).

4. Merriam-Webster Online, s.v. "insight," http://www.merriam -webster.com/dictionary/insight (August 29, 2013).

Chapter Four—The Principle of Publishing: Writing Preserves and Proliferates Vision

1. "From Academic to Professional Writing," Cleveland State University, http://www.csuohio.edu/academic/writingcenter/WAC/academic toprofessional.html (accessed August 30, 2013).

2. "Quotes About Readers," Goodreads, http://www.goodreads .com/quotes/tag/readers (accessed August 30, 2013).

Chapter Five—The Principle of Perpetuation: Perpetuated Truth Has Infinite Transformative Power

1. "Alex Haley," Kunta Kinte-Alex Haley Foundation, Inc., http:// www.kintehaley.org/testsite/alex-haley/ (accessed August 30, 2013).

2. Ibid.

3. http://www.museum.tv/eotvsection.php?entrycode=roots

4. Ibid.

5. Strong's, s.v. "ba'ar" (OT 874).

6. "Theodore Hesburgh Quotes," ThinkExist.com, http://think exist.com/quotation/the_very_essence_of_leadership_is_that _you_have/225727.html (accessed August 30, 2013).

7. Seth Godin, "Frequency, repetition and the power of saying it more than once," http://sethgodin.typepad.com/seths_blog/2013/04/frequency-repetition-and-the-power-of-saying-it-more-than-once.html (accessed August 30, 2013).

8. Ibid.

9. "Quotable Quote," Goodreads, http://www.goodreads.com/quotes/426122-having-a-vision-is-not-enough-it-must-be-combined (August 30, 2013).

10. "John Maxwell Quotes," ThinkExist.com, http://thinkexist.com/quotation/where_there_is_no_hope_in_the_future-there_is_no/13870.html (August 30, 2013).

Chapter Six—The Principle of Process:
God's Process Yields God's Promised Vision

1. *The Free Dictionary,* s.v. "process," http://www.thefreedictionary.com/process (accessed August 30, 2013).

2. Charles Francis Potter, "Time in Bible Times," *Journal of the Royal Astronomical Society of Canada, Vol. 35, 165,* http://articles.adsabs.harvard.edu//full/1941JRASC..35..163P/0000165.000.html (accessed August 30, 2013).

3. *Wikipedia, the Free Encyclopedia,* s.v. "kairos," en.wikipedia.org/wiki/Kairos (accessed August 30, 2013).

4. J. Oswald Sanders, *Spiritual Leadership: Principles of Excellence for Every Believer* (Chicago: Moody Bible Institute, 1994), 56.

5. Biblesoft's New Exhaustive Strong's, s.v. "klepto," (NT 2813).

6. Ibid., s.v. "thuo," (NT 2380).

7. *The NAS New Testament Greek Lexicon,* BibleStudyTools.com, s.v. "martureo," (NT 3140), http://www.biblestudytools.com/lexicons/greek/nas/martureo.html (accessed August 30, 2013).

8. Adelaide A. Pollard, "Have Thine Own Way, Lord," 1907, public domain.

Chapter Seven—The Principle of Patience:
Possessing Vision Requires Patience

1. "Winners Never Quit and Quitters Never Win," sermonsearch, sermon by Dr. James Merritt, "Home Sweet Home," http://www.sermonsearch.com/sermon-outlines/20828/winners-never-quit-and-quitters-never-win-longsuffering-4-of-9/ (August 30, 2013).

2. "What is apartheid?" Yahoo.answers, http://answers.yahoo.com/question/index?qid=1006041004016 (accessed August 30, 2013).

3. W.E. Vine, *Vine's Expository Dictionary of Biblical Words* (Nashville: Thomas Nelson, 1985), s.v. "makrothumia" (NT: 3115).

4. "Aristotle Quotes…," Goodreads, http://www.goodreads.com/quotes/16892-patience-is-bitter-but-its-fruit-is-sweet (August 30, 2013).

5. "Henri J.M. Nouwen," Goodreads, http://www.goodreads.com/author/show/4837.Henri_J_M_Nouwen (August 30, 2013).

Chapter Eight—The Principle of Passion:
You Are Driven by Your Heart's Desire

1. Kathryn Spink, *Mother Teresa: An Authorized Biography* (New York: HarperCollins, 2011), 6.

2. "Mother Teresa," bio.True Story, http://www.biography.com/people/mother-teresa-9504160?page=2 (August 30, 2013).

3. Ibid., http://www.biography.com/people/mother-teresa-9504160?page=3.

4. "Mother Teresa Quotes," Goodreads, http://www.goodreads .com/author/quotes/838305.Mother_Teresa (August 30, 2013).

5. "Mother Teresa," bio.True Story, http://www.biography.com/ people/mother-teresa-9504160?page=3 (accessed August 30, 2013).

Chapter Nine—The Principle of Productivity: Right Motives Produce Right Results

1. Dictionary.com. *Dictionary.com Unabridged*, Random House, Inc., s.v. "productivity," http://dictionary.reference.com/browse/ productivity (accessed: August 30, 2013).

2. "Life, the Truth, and Being Free Quotes," Goodreads, http:// www.goodreads.com/work/quotes/14708444-life-the-truth -and-being-free?page=6 (August 30, 2013).

3. R.C. Sproul, "Time Well Spent: Right Now Counts Forever," *Tabletalk* (September, 1997). Article is excerpted at C.J. Mahaney, "Time. Redeemed." Dec. 9, 2008, Sovereign Grace Ministries, http://www.sovereigngraceministries.org/blogs/cj-mahaney/ post/time-redeemed.aspx (accessed August 30, 2013).

4. "C.G. Young," Goodreads, http://www.goodreads.com/author/ show/38285.C_G_Jung (August 30, 2013).

Chapter Ten—The Principle of Perseverance: Never Let Go of Your Vision!

1. *The Free Dictionary*, s.v. "perseverance," http://www.thefreediction ary.com/perseverance, (accessed September 2, 2013).

About the Author

Dr. Teresa Hairston is a woman of leadership and legacy. She is nationally known and respected as the founder of *Gospel Today* magazine. She started the publication in 1989 with an investment of only $300, while working two jobs and being a single mother to three young children. *Gospel Today* grew to become the longest-running and most widely distributed Christian lifestyle magazine in history. In 2011, she retired from *Gospel Today* and passed this great legacy to her son.

In 1994, Dr. Hairston founded The Gospel Heritage Foundation, which celebrates and educates regarding worship. Each year, thousands from across the world attend the annual Gospel Heritage Praise & Worship Conference, which has become the genre's leading international praise and worship conference.

Dr. Hairston is an ordained elder, preacher of the Gospel, dynamic international teacher, and author of the book *How to Pursue Your Purpose*. She is single, lives in Atlanta, and is the doting grandmother of five.

Email: drhairstongt@aol.com

Website: teresahairston.com

Ministry address: P O Box 800, Fairburn, GA 30213

Ministry phone: 770.866.2427